LEARNING TO DRIVE

LEARNING
TO
DRIVE

And Other Life Stories

~

Katha Pollitt

RANDOM HOUSE
New York

Published in the United States by Random House, an imprint of The Random
House Publishing Group, a division of Random House, Inc., New York.

RANDOM HOUSE and colophon are registered trademarks of Random House, Inc.

"Learning to Drive" and "Webstalker"
were originally published in *The New Yorker*.

Grateful acknowledgment is made to Elizabeth Hauser for permission
to reprint "Growing Up" by Marchette Chute, originally published
in *Child Life* magazine. Reprinted by permission.

LIBRARY OF CONGRESS CATALOGING-IN-PUBLICATION DATA
Pollitt, Katha.
Learning to drive: and other life stories / Katha Pollitt.
p. cm.
ISBN 978-1-4000-6332-1
I. Title.
PS3566.O533L43 2007
813'.54—dc22   2007008383

Printed in the United States of America on acid-free paper

www.atrandom.com

4 6 8 9 7 5

Book design by Casey Hampton

IN MEMORY OF MY PARENTS

Leanora Levine Pollitt (1925–1979)

Basil Riddiford Pollitt (1919–2005)

CONTENTS

LEARNING TO DRIVE

LEARNING TO DRIVE

"OVER THERE, THE RED JEEP. PARK!" BEN, MY gentle Filipino driving instructor, has suddenly become severe, abrupt, commanding. A slight man, he now looms bulkily in his seat; his usually soft voice has acquired a threatening edge. In a scenario that we have repeated dozens of times, and that has kinky overtones I don't even want to think about, he is pretending to be the test examiner, barking out orders as we tool along the streets above Columbia University in the early morning. I am impersonating the would-be licensee, obediently carrying out instructions. "Pull out when you are ready!" "Right turn!" "Left turn at the intersection!" "Straight!" "All right, Ms. Pollitt, pull over." He doesn't even need to say the words. From the rueful look on his once again kindly face I know that I have failed.

What did I do wrong this time? Did I run a red light, miss a stop sign, fail to notice one of the many bicyclists who sneak into my blind spot whenever I go into reverse? Each of these mistakes means automatic failure. Or did I fail on points? Five for parallel-parking more than fourteen inches from the curb and not successfully fixing it, ten for rolling when I paused for the woman with the stroller (but at least I saw her! I saw her!), fifteen for hesitating in the intersection, so that a driver in a car with New Jersey plates honked and gave me the finger? This time it was points, Ben tells me: in our five-minute practice test I racked up sixty. New York State allows you thirty.

"Observation, Kahta, observation! This is your weakness." This truth hangs in the air like mystical advice from an Asian sage in a martial-arts movie. "That, and lining up too far away when you go to park."

The clock on the dashboard reads 7:47. We will role-play the test repeatedly during my two-hour lesson. I will fail every time.

~

Observation is my weakness. I did not realize that my mother was a secret drinker. I did not realize that the man I lived with, my soul mate, made for me in Marxist heaven, was a dedicated philanderer, that the drab colleague he insinuated into our social life was his long-standing secret girlfriend, or that the young art critic he mocked as silly and second-rate was being groomed as my replacement. I noticed that our apartment was becoming a grunge palace, with books and papers collecting dust on every surface and kitty litter crunching underfoot. I observed—very good, Kahta!—that I was spending many hours in my study, engaged in arcane e-mail debates with strangers, that I had gained twenty-five pounds in our seven years together and could not fit into many of my clothes. I realized it was not likely that the unfamiliar pink-and-black-striped bikini panties in the clean-clothes basket were the result, as he claimed, of a simple laundry room mix-up. But all this awareness was like the impending danger in one of those slow-motion dreams of paralysis, information that could not be processed. It was like seeing the man with the suitcase step off the curb and driving forward anyway.

~

I am a fifty-two-year-old woman who has yet to get a driver's license. I'm not the only older woman who can't legally drive—Ben recently had a sixty-five-year-old student who took the test four times before she passed—but perhaps I am the only fifty-two-year-old feminist writer in this situation. How did this happen to me? For decades, all around me, women were laying claim to forbidden manly skills—how to fix the furnace, perform brain surgery, hunt seals, have sex without love. Only I, it seems, stood still, growing, if anything, more helpless as the machines in my life increased in both number and complexity. When I was younger, not driving had overtones of New York hipness— growing up in the city, I didn't learn to drive because I went to an old-fashioned private girls' school that taught Latin and how to make a linzer torte instead of dorky suburban boy subjects like driver's ed. There was something beatnik, intellectual, European about being disconnected from the car culture: the rest of America might deliquesce into one big strip mall, but New York City would remain a little outpost of humane civilization, an enclave of ancient modes of transportation—the subway, the bus, the taxi, the bicycle, the foot. Having a car in New York was not liberation but enslavement to the alternate-side-of-the-street parking ritual, to constant risk of theft. Still, my family always had a car—a Buick, a Rambler, some big, lumbering masculine make. My father would sit in it and smoke and listen to the ball game in the soft summer evening, when he and my mother had had a fight.

~

"I am trying so hard to help you, Kahta," Ben says. "I was thinking about you after yesterday's lesson—I feel perhaps I am failing you as your teacher." In a lifetime in and out of academia, I have never before heard a teacher suggest that his student's difficulties might have something to do with him. The truth is, Ben is a natural pedagogue—organized, patient, engaged with his subject, and always looking for new ways to explain some tricky point. Sometimes he illustrates what I should have done by using a pair of toy cars, and I can see the little boy he once was—intent, happy, lost in play. Sometimes he makes up analogies:

"Kahta, how do you know if you've put in enough salt and pepper when you are making beef stew?"

"Um, you taste it?"

"Riiight, you taste it. So: what do you do if you've lost track of which way the car is pointing when you parallel-park?"

"I dunno, Ben. You taste it?"

"You just let the car move back a tiny bit and see which way it goes! You taste the direction! Then you—"

"Correct the seasonings?"

"Riiight . . . you adjust!"

~

Because it takes me a while every morning to focus on the task at hand, Ben and I have fallen into the habit of long lessons—we drive for two hours, sometimes even three. We go up to Washington Heights and drive around the winding, hilly roads of Fort Tryon Park, around the narrow crooked Tudoresque streets near Castle Village. What a beautiful neighborhood! we exclaim. Look at that Art Deco subway station entrance! Look at those Catholic schoolgirls in front of Mother Cabrini High, in those incredibly cute, sexy plaid uniforms! I am careful to stop for the old rabbi; I pause and make eye contact with the mother herding her two little boys. It's like another, secret New York up here, preserved from the 1940s, in which jogging yuppies in electric-blue spandex look like time travelers from the future among the staid elderly burghers walking their dogs along the leafy sidewalks overlooking the Hudson. In that New York, the one without road-raging New Jersey drivers or sneaky cyclists, in which life is lived at twenty miles per hour, I feel sure I could have gotten my license with no trouble. I could have been living here all along, commuting to a desk job in midtown and coming out of the Art Deco entrance at dusk, feeling like I was in the country, with sweet-smelling creamy pink magnolias all around me.

~

I spend more time with Ben than any other man just now. There are days when, except for an exchange of smiles and hellos with Mohammed at the newsstand and my supper-time phone call with a man I am seeing who lives in London, Ben is the only man I talk to. In a way he's per-fect—his use of the double brake is protective without being infantilizing, his corrections are firm but never con-descending or judgmental, he spares my feelings but tells the truth if asked. ("Let's say I took the test tomorrow, Ben. What are my chances?" "I'd say maybe fifty-fifty." I must be pretty desperate—those don't seem like such bad odds to me.) He's a big improvement on my former boyfriend, who told a mutual friend that he was leaving me because I didn't have a driver's license, spent too much time on e-mail, and had failed in seven years to read Anton Pannekoek's *Workers' Councils* and other classics of the ultra-Left. Ben would never leave me because I don't have a driver's license. Quite the reverse. Sometimes I feel sad to think that these lessons must one day come to an end—will I ever see those little streets again, or drive around Fort Tryon Park in the spring? "Will you still be my teacher, Ben, after I get my license, so I can learn how to drive on the highway?" Ben promises that he will always be there for me, and I believe him.

~

In at least one way, I am like the other older women learning to drive: I am here because I have lost my man. Most women in my condition are widows or divorcees who spent their lives under Old World rules, in which driving was a male prerogative and being ferried about a female privilege. My boyfriend's mother lived in the wilds of Vermont for years with her Marxist-intellectual husband. With the puritanical zeal for which German Jews are famous, she kept the house spotless, grew all their fruits and vegetables, and raised her son to be a world-class womanizer—while earning a Ph.D. that would enable her to support her husband's life of reading and writing and, of course, driving. She didn't learn to drive until after his death, when she was over sixty. To hear her tell it now, the whole process took five minutes. When she asked if I'd got my license yet—which she did every time we spoke—she adopted a tone of intense and invasive concern. It was as if she were asking me if the Thorazine had started to work.

~

Ben is not my first driving teacher. When I was twenty-seven and about to spend a summer in New Hampshire, I took lessons from Mike, a young and rather obnoxious Italian American. "That's okay, I can walk to the curb from here," he would say when I parked too wide. He liked to pass off as his own bons mots from the late-night talk shows. "Hey, did you hear about the funeral home on Columbus Avenue? It's called Death 'n Stuff." After a month of lessons I took the test in the Bronx and didn't even notice that I'd hit a stop sign when I parked. Automatic failure. Mike drove me back to Manhattan in hostile silence and didn't call to schedule a lesson again. Ben would never do that.

That was it for driving until four years ago, when I bought a house on the Connecticut shore and signed up for lessons with an instructor I'll call Tom. He was Italian American also, middle-aged, overweight, and rather sweet, but liable to spells of anger and gloom, as if he had raised too many sons like Mike. On bad days, as we drove around the back roads and shopping centers of Clinton and Madison and Guilford, Tom would seethe about the criminal propensities of the black inhabitants of New Haven. On good days, he liked to talk about religion, about which he had some interesting theories. For example, he believed that Jesus Christ was a space alien, which would explain a lot—the star of Bethlehem, the walking on water, the Resurrection. Besides, Tom said, "No human being could be that good." He made me memorize his special method of sliding backward into a parking space, failed to impress upon me the existence of blind spots, and, like his predecessor, lost all interest in me when I flunked the road test.

I should have signed up to take the test again immediately—hadn't the examiner said that all I needed was more confidence? Instead I spent several years driving around the shoreline with my boyfriend in the passenger seat, as

Connecticut law permits. He had special methods too—for instance, on tricky maneuvers at an intersection he would urge me to "be one car" with the car in front, which means just do what that car is doing. Ben looked a little puzzled when I told him about that. He thinks you should take more charge of your automotive destiny—what if the car in front is doing something really stupid? "Listen to your inner voice," he tells me when I continue going back as I parallel-park, even though I know I am about to go over the curb, which is an automatic failure on the test. "You are right, Kahta, you knew! Your inner voice is trying to help you!" You can't listen to your inner voice and be one car, too, is what Ben is getting at.

What was my boyfriend thinking, I wonder, when we cruised Route 1, shuttling between our little house and the bookstore, the movie theater, Al Forno for pizza, the Clam Castle for lobster rolls, visiting Hammonasset Beach to watch the twilight spread softly over that long expanse of shining sand? Was he daydreaming about the young art critic, thinking about how later he would go off on his bicycle and call the drab colleague from the pay phone at the Stop & Shop? Was he thinking what a drag it was to have a girl-friend who couldn't pass a simple road test, even in small-town Connecticut, who did not care about the value-price transformation problem and who never once woke him up with a blow job, despite being told many times that this was what all men wanted? Perhaps the young art critic is a bet-ter girlfriend on these and other scores, and he no longer feels the need for other women. Or perhaps the deception was the exciting part for him, and he will betray her, too, which is, of course, what I hope.

Now as I drive around upper Manhattan with Ben I spend a lot of time ignoring the road and asking myself, If I had gotten my driver's license, would my boyfriend have left me? Perhaps my procrastination about the road test was symbolic to him of other resistances and fears and obliviousness. "In the end," he said as he was leaving, ostensibly to "be alone" but actually, as I soon discovered, to join the young art critic on Fire Island, "our relationship revolves around you." "That's not true!" I wept. He also said, "Every day you wake up happy and cheerful and I'm lonely and miserable." "No I don't!" I stormed. He continued, "You never read the books I recommend." I pointed out that I was reading one such book at that very moment—*A World Full of Gods: Pagans, Jews and Christians in the Roman Empire,* by Keith Hopkins. "I mean serious political books," he said. "Books that are important to me." Okay, point taken. Then came the coup de grace: "I finally saw that you would never change."

What can you say to that? Change what? If I had read Anton Pannekoek's *Workers' Councils,* if I had given up e-mail for blow jobs at dawn, if I had got my license, would we still be together, driving north to buy daylilies at White Flower Farm while learnedly analyzing the Spartacist Revolution of 1919? Perhaps, it occurs to me, as a demented cabbie cuts me off on Riverside Drive, it's a lucky thing I didn't get my license. I would still be living with a womanizer, a liar, a cheat, a manipulator, a maniac, a psychopath. Maybe my incompetence protected me.

New York State puts out an official booklet of rules of the road, but there are no textbooks that teach the art of driving itself. The closest is a tattered test result, much passed about by teachers, from the days when examiners filled out a form by hand. "I know his mother!" I exclaim when Ben gives me a copy. The test happens to belong to a young writer, sometimes written up in gossip columns as a member of an all-boy fast crowd. "You see, Kahta! He failed to anticipate the actions of others. He didn't stop for pedestrians. And he forgot his turn signals, too." Ben shakes his head sorrowfully over the young writer's terrible score—seventy points off! I find this failure oddly cheering.

Mostly, though, driving is a skill transmitted by word of mouth, by experience, one to one. In this, it resembles few human activities, most of which can be learned from a book, or so we tell ourselves—think how many sex manuals are published every year, not to mention those educational sex videos advertised in high-toned literary publications, aimed at people who were fantasizing about Mr. Rochester and Mr. Darcy while their classmates were steaming up the windows of their parents' cars. My boyfriend and I bought a pocket-sized edition of *The Joy of Sex*, intending to go through it page by page, like the lovers in Robert Hellenga's *The Fall of a Sparrow*. But somehow we never got past "Serbian Bird-song," which was just making love in the morning, which we had been doing all along. That was another accusation he flung at me the day he left: "You bought *The Joy of Sex*, but you just put it in a drawer!" "Why was it my job to improve our sex life?" I retorted. "You could have opened that book anytime." I suppose the truth was that, given his multiple exhausting commitments, he didn't need to.

⌒

Sometimes when I am driving I become suddenly bewildered—it is as if I had never turned left at an intersection or parallel-parked before. How do I know which lane to drive into? How many times have I turned the wheel while angling back into my parking space? I become hot and flushed and totally confused, and for some reason I keep turning the wheel until it's maxed out and then look frantically at Ben.

"What do I do now, Ben? How far back do I turn it? How do I know when it's where it's supposed to be?"

"Beef stew, Kahta! Remember?"

"You mean I should just let it go back a tiny bit to see where it will go?"

"Riiight. You see, you are learning! Beef-stew it!"

But what if I get my license and I have one of these episodes of befuddlement when I'm alone at the wheel? Ben often has to remind me not to zone out, as I so frequently do even while I'm warning myself to stay focused. For example, I'll be staring at the red light, determined not to let my mind wander, and then I start wondering why red means "stop" and green means "go." Is there some optic science behind this color scheme? Is it arbitrary? Perhaps it derives from an ancient custom, the way the distance between railroad tracks is derived from the distance between the wheels on Roman carts. I think how sad and romantic streetlights look when blurred in the rain, and how before electricity no one could experience that exact romantic sadness, because nothing could have looked like that. I savor the odd fact that a street scene that seems so old-fashioned now is actually a product of modernity, and then it hits me that this is the sort of idea my boyfriend was always having, and I wonder if I will ever have my mind back wholly to myself or if I will always feel invaded, abandoned, bereft.

"Kahta," Ben says gently, "the light has been green for some time now. Please, go!"

~

My boyfriend used to joke that I had missed my chance to rid myself of my former husband forever by failing to run him over while an unlicensed, inexperienced driver. Actually, my ex and I get on very well. He's an excellent father, and when I have a computer problem he helps me over the phone, although he refuses to come over and fix the machine himself. Now when I am careering up Riverside Drive I sometimes fantasize that I see my boyfriend and his new girlfriend in the crosswalk. I wave my arms helplessly as the car, taking on a life of its own, homes into them like a magnet smashing into a bar of iron. Sometimes I put the drab colleague in the crosswalk, too, and run all three of them down. No jury would believe it had been an accident, although Ben would surely testify in my favor. I'd go to jail for decades, and the case would be made into a movie for one of those cable channels for women: *Out of Control: The Katha Pollitt Story*. What a disappointing end to my struggle for personal growth! Yet one not without consolations: in jail, after all, I would not need to drive. I could settle into comfy middle age, reorganizing the prison library and becoming a lesbian.

~

Twelve years ago, I saw a therapist who urged me to learn to drive to set an example for my daughter, who was then a toddler. She pointed out that my mother had never learned to drive and waited, in silence, as they do, for me to see a connection. Well, it's obvious isn't it? My mother was a kind of professional helpless person. If she was alone in the house and couldn't open a jar, she would take it to the corner bar and ask one of the drunks to open it for her. "Don't be like your mother," my father would say in exasperation when I displayed particular ineptitude in the face of the physical world. And except for the matter of driving, I'm not. I'm meaner and stronger and I'm not drinking myself to death. I own a special tool for twisting recalcitrant jar lids. Unlike my mother, I can time cooking a meal so that the rice, the meat, and the vegetables all come out ready together. But it's true that my culinary skills deteriorated precipitously while I was living with my former boyfriend, a fabulous cook who had once prepared dinner for the mayor of Bologna and who took over the kitchen the minute he moved in. Gradually I forgot what I knew and lost the confidence to try new recipes; nor did I ever learn to use any of the numerous appliances he collected: the espresso machine with cappuccino attachment, the Cuisinart mini-prep, or the deep-fat fryer he bought the day after I said I was going on a diet.

My father made my mother sign up with a driving school. In fact, she was taking a lesson at the very moment word came over the car radio that President Kennedy had been shot. She claimed that this event so traumatized her that she could never get back behind the wheel. I didn't believe her—she'd never liked JFK, who had invaded Cuba and brought the world to the brink of nuclear war with the missile crisis. I think she was just afraid, the way I am— afraid of killing myself, afraid of killing someone else. I was fourteen when my mother gave up on her license, the same age my daughter is now, but I give myself bonus points, because I'm still taking lessons. "You can do it, Mom," my daughter calls to me over her cereal when I dash out the door for my lesson. "Just keep your hands on the wheel." In a weak moment, I mentioned to her that sometimes at a red light I forget and put my hands in my lap—that would earn a warning from the examiner right there. I am trying to set her a good example, as that long-ago therapist urged—the example of a woman who does not fall apart because the man she loved lied to her every single minute of their life together and then left her for a woman young enough to be his daughter. "I'm going to be a little obsessed for a while," I told her. "I'm going to spend a lot of time talking on the phone with my friends and I may cry sometimes, but basically I'm fine. Also, I'm going on a huge diet, and I don't want any teenage anorexia from you."

"Mom!" She gave me the parents-are-weird eye roll. The truth is, though, she's proud of me. When I do something new—figure out what's wrong with the computer without having to call my ex-husband, or retake the big study I vacated for my boyfriend when he moved in, or give away my schlumpy old fat clothes and buy a lot of beautiful velvet pants and tops in deep jewel colors—she pumps her arm and says, *"Mujer de metal!"*

~

Ben is not just a great driving instructor; he is an interesting conversationalist. On our long lessons, he tells me all about growing up in Manila: the beauty of going to Mass with his mother every day, and how sad it was to lose touch with his sisters when they married and became part of their husbands' families. When he says he prays for me to pass the driving test I am so moved—I picture him surrounded by clouds of incense and tropical flowers, dressed in ornate robes, like the Infant of Prague. Ben thinks a lot about being Asian. He feels proud whenever Asians succeed, like when we drive through a middle-class neighborhood and you can see Asians are living there. But he's got his stereotypes. "She's Korean," he'll announce about the gray-haired pedestrian crossing the street. "The long strides, the wooden face." Or "He's Japanese—you can tell because he looks so mean."

"Do you think I'm a weird Asian, Kahta?" Ben asks me. "Not at all," I say firmly, although how would I tell? I know plenty of Asian Americans, but Ben is practically the only Asian-raised-in-Asia I know. "You don't think Asians are boring, Kahta?" He tells me Asians repress their feelings, especially anger—which makes me wonder if he is secretly angry at me for making so many mistakes—and that Westerners don't understand their jokes. I tell him mostly I know about Asians from movies and books—for example, ancient Chinese poetry and the novels of Shusaku Endo. "What about the Kama Sutra?" he asks, and we laugh and insist we've never read it, never even looked at it, and then we laugh some more, because we know we are both lying. "See that pedestrian? He's Bob Marley's son," Ben says, pointing to a handsome young black man with short dreadlocks who's entering Riverside Church. And while I am wondering how Ben would know that—maybe Bob Jr. took lessons from him?—he cracks up. "You believed me!" Ben can be quite a humorist. And yet sometimes I worry about him, going home after a long day to his studio apartment in Floral Park, Long Island. He's forty-four, and it will be years before he can marry his fiancée, who is forty and a schoolteacher back in the Philippines. When he goes home, he has three beers, which seems like a lot to drink alone. ("It used to be two, now three.") If I believed in God I would pray for him—to get his own driving school, and be able to bring his fiancée over and move with her to a nice two-bedroom in Castle Village, on the side that looks out over the river.

Some mornings, I know I mystify Ben. "Did you notice that hazard, Kahta? That double-parked SUV?" I admit I have no idea what he's talking about. "Always look ahead, Kahta. Look at the big picture, not just what's right in front of you. Observation!" Other days, though, I know I'm making progress. I zip up West End Avenue, enjoying the fresh green of the old plane trees and the early-morning quiet. I perform the physical work of driving, but with a kind of Zen dispersal of attention, so that as I am keeping an even pace and staying in my lane I am also noticing the bakery van signaling a right turn, and the dog walker hesitating on the curb with his cluster of chows and retrievers. A block ahead, I see a school bus stopping in front of the same old Italianate apartment building where my daughter, my boyfriend, and I used to wait for the bus when she was in elementary school, and I am already preparing to be careful and cautious because you never know when a little child might dart out into the street.

At that moment, it seems possible that I will pass the driving test, if not this time, then the next. One morning soon, I will put my license in my pocket, I will get into the car, turn the key, and enjoy the rumbly throat-clearing sound of the engine starting up. I will flick the turn signal down, so it makes that satisfying, precise click. I will pull out when I am ready and drive—it doesn't even matter where. I will make eye contact with pedestrians, I will be aware of cyclists coming up behind me; the smooth and confident trajectory of my vehicle will wordlessly convey to cabbies and Jersey drivers that they should keep at least three car lengths away, and more should it be raining. I will listen to my inner voice, I will look ahead to get the big picture, I will observe. I will beef-stew it. I will be *mujer de metal.*

WEBSTALKER

AFTER MY BOYFRIEND LEFT ME, I WENT A LITTLE crazy for a while. By day, I could pass for normal, as that concept is broadly understood on the Upper West Side, where I live—I sat at my desk, I took long furious walks in Riverside Park rehearsing all the terrible things I would say to him as he lay stricken with something rare and painful, I wandered through Zabar's looking for kitchen things to replace the ones he took when he moved out. What kind of person walks out the door after seven years with a wooden spoon, a spatula, a whisk? For months, I would find myself in the middle of a recipe only to discover that some basic, necessary implement was missing. But at night, after my daughter was in bed, I would settle myself at the computer with a cup of coffee, and till one or two in the morning I would browse the Internet, searching for information about him. Except "browse" is much too placid and leisured a word—a cow browses in a meadow, a reader browses in a library for a novel to take home for the weekend. What I did fell between zeal and monomania. I was like Javert, hunting him through the sewers of cyberspace, moving from link to link in the dark, like Spider-Man flinging himself by a filament over the shadowy chasm between one roof and another. "Are you Webstalking him?" a friend in her twenties asked over coffee. I hadn't known there was a word for what I was doing.

At first I felt guilty, as if somehow he could know. After all, if an e-mail program can tell you whether your message has been opened, maybe a search engine can tell you that someone is checking you out. Still, I would plug his name into Google, Lycos, HotBot, Alta Vista, and up would pop, in distilled, allusive, elliptical form, like a haiku or a mathematical curve, everything I should have known: the life behind my life. Out of a soup or cloud composed of book reviews, publishers' notices, conference announcements, course assignments, Listserv postings, and tiny mentions and stray references embedded in documents devoted to some quite distant theme, a person would slowly condense, like someone approaching out of a fog who at first looks as if he were made out of fog, only darker. There on my screen glowed the programs of academic gatherings he had attended going back for a decade: the same female names appeared over and over entwined with his in panel announcements. Why hadn't it struck me as odd that his "best friend," a professor of English literature, was the respondent for papers he gave at conferences on art history and philosophy? Was I even aware that they attended these events together? And what about the philosopher he'd been seeing, I'd recently discovered, when we'd started dating, and the art historian who'd called all the time and then, one day, stopped calling? They were on those panels, too. I had been so out of it!

But of course I already knew that. After he left, I walked around my semi-dismantled apartment and interrogated the ghost-squares on the empty walls. Were any of the pictures I had lived with gifts from women he had romanced? The cat cartoon? The charcoal of sad-looking trees? A splashy abstractionist painter, as a thank-you for his writing about her work, had given him a big acrylic of black stripes laid over red swirls, like flames billowing behind an iron grille. He'd hung it in the living room and refused to take it down when I said I hated it, that it reminded me of the gates of Hell. He had left only one art work behind—a colorful picture of two ambiguously sexed people embracing, by a jolly, tough-talking artist we had socialized with when her child and mine were small. I called her up and told her I had belatedly come to conclude that my boyfriend had had affairs during our years together and I didn't want to keep her picture if she had slept with him. "I never saw his genitals," she said cheerfully—she'd just mooned around with him in coffee shops. He had told her that I accepted his need for other women, so it didn't seem fair to hate her. Besides, she'd turned him down. I left her picture up in the bathroom, next to the towel rack.

Still, it astonished me that she'd believed that business about my permitting his philandering. The only people who seem to know such women firsthand are the men who are cheating on them. You never hear a woman say, "Whatever George wants is fine with me—I just want him to be happy!" No woman has ever passed on to another the riveting news that Miriam understands that Joe needs variety. It is only men who seem to possess this bit of intimate knowledge, which apparently is so instantly credible, so obviously true, that no one ever asks the woman herself about it. What was it about me, I wondered, that made people accept his story? Perhaps I emitted a sort of wan victim-aura, like someone sitting alone in a Greek diner. Or perhaps people just couldn't believe I was so oblivious. After all, I was intelligent, I was a New Yorker, I was alive.

But, then, how well does anyone really know anyone else? My boyfriend used to make fun of people who gave money to museums and universities—he claimed that they just wanted to feel important by connecting themselves to elite bourgeois institutions. Yet, according to Google, in 1995 he made a donation to the Weidner Center for the Performing Arts, at the University of Wisconsin in Green Bay, a cultural venue that he never mentioned and that I was not even aware existed. Or was it someone else? After all, he was not the only person with his name. There was his father, the Marxist theoretician. Most of my search results were about him—fans from Canada to Korea posted his works far and wide. While living with his son, I had found his books impenetrably technical and Teutonic, but through sheer familiarity I was coming to enjoy his gloomy, sardonic turn of mind, his doom-laden pronouncements in which the certainty that he was right was given a poignant cast by his awareness that few were listening and fewer agreed. I found myself nodding in sympathy as I reencountered his work. "Capitalism," he wrote, "has nowhere to go but to its death." You can't argue with that. There were also numerous mentions of a property lawyer in Australia who was active in his children's school, and an accountant on the Isle of Wight who placed well in the 1999 North Drove Doddle amateur rowing competition, and who may or may not be the man of the same name who was an avid promoter of shove ha'penny, an old English game. It was barely possible, but most unlikely, that my boyfriend, sometimes under his name and sometimes under assorted misspellings of it, posted brief rude messages in idiomatic French on a Web site devoted to the work of the "bad boy" filmmaker Leos Carax (*"bojarksi arrete de boire la tasse"*; *"bah alors!"*). But that person did not sound like someone who cared about bringing *Fiddler on the Roof* to the Midwest. Perhaps the Weidner donor was one of those rare people who are unknown to the Net: someone with no e-mail, no Web site or Web page, no blog or—barring that one donation—connections with anyone who has such things. Perhaps he still wrote letters on a typewriter and posted them at the mailbox on the corner when he walked the dog in the crisp Wisconsin morning. If only I had met him instead of my boyfriend! Unless, of course, he was my boyfriend.

Mostly, though, I Webstalked him to find out what he

was up to now. I knew when he went to Philadelphia for the College Art Association meeting, when his essay on eighteenth-century art-critical terminology was assigned in a class at Essex University, when he sent a flattering e-mail to the Web site of a conceptual artist whose work consisted of reading *Das Kapital* out loud in dozens of obscure foreign languages and invited this artist to be involved in a book he was "producing" with his new girlfriend. I don't know what made me saddest: that they were cowriting, or at least coproducing—whatever that is—a book? That he was seeking out this half-baked poseur? That he prefaced his girlfriend's name with "critic," the way it would appear in *Time?* Clearly, his prose style had deteriorated since he left me— the man I'd loved would surely have written "the critic," which is the correct and elegant usage.

~

I've always believed in the Nero Wolfe theory of knowledge. You can just sit quietly in your room—according to Pascal, the activity that if practiced more assiduously would free humanity from most of its troubles, but that was before e-mail—and through sheer mental effort force the tiniest snippets of information to yield the entire story of which they are a fragment, because the whole truth is contained in every particle of it, the way every one of our cells contains our DNA. Thus, each new search result drove me wild with excitement: maybe this would be the link that would, properly understood, reveal all. Late at night, sipping my cold coffee, I saw the Web as a parallel world, the verbal equivalent of the life we live, a shimmering net of information that exactly and completely corresponds to the world. It was like something a medieval rabbi might conjure up out of the Kabbalah; a magical set of propositions that acted as a mirror of reality and perhaps even allowed you to control it and change it. It was as if I would be able to actually watch him in real time—giving a talk, teaching a class, making dinner, making love—if I could only find that final link that would make the parallel proposition-world complete. Unfortunately, I wasn't very technologically adept. I kept running into the limits of my skills. What, for example, is a PDF? Some pieces of seemingly routine information I was unable to find, although I felt sure they had to be there, somewhere, behind the brick wall of my incompetence: his course schedule (did it still match that of the "best friend"?), his new girlfriend's undergraduate college or hometown or birth date. I knew where he lived, because his girlfriend was listed in the phone book, but did they have cats? Did he take her to the restaurants we had discovered together? I kicked myself for not having written down his Social Security and credit-card numbers. "You don't have those?" my young friend asked, surprised. She had a whole ID file on her boyfriend, "just in case."

How could I find out more? I considered replying to one of those spam ads advertising detective software, like the "Banned CD" that supposedly helps you turn up all sorts of hidden legal and financial information about people. But those e-mails had a threatening, paranoid tone; responding might connect me with sinister people who would show up at my apartment. Besides, it was one thing to stay up half the night going through the archives of obscure leftist Listservs and e-mailing this or that woman to ask if she had ever slept with the man I had been living with. (Amazingly, they all wrote back nice notes affirming that they had, except for one, who sent a huffy e-mail saying that it was none of my business. In other words, yes.) It was another thing to bring in professional help. Then, too, the Banned CD cost $19.95, and to pay for information would be proof of serious dementia.

Instead, I tried to break into his e-mail. I had his password—"marxist"—or did I? When I'd asked him what his password was, a few months before he left, he had cleared his throat and paused. I'd attributed this hesitation to modesty—he was embarrassed to claim such a heroic identity, or to use such a large, noble, world-historical word for such a trivial purpose. But perhaps he'd hesitated because he was afraid I would use it and find out his secrets—or was thinking up a fake password so that I couldn't. In any case, "marxist" didn't work when I tried to access his mail through mail2web.com; nor did any of the other words I tried: "marxism," "marx," "karlmarx," "engels," "communist," "communism," "pannekoek," "korsch," "luxemburg," "luxembourg," "belgium," "chocolate," "godiva," "naked," "breast," "cunnilingus," "fellatio," and the names of our cats, his new girlfriend, his mother's dead golden retriever. My password is "secret," which is so obvious that e-mail programs cite it as the exact word not to choose, but I like it because it is a philosophical pun—"secret" as a secret password, the word that is also the thing itself. I noticed he didn't ask for my password, but I told him anyway.

He had accused me of being addicted to the Internet, and he was right. I spent hours every day following the news and surfing from one odd Web site to another. I joined Listservs all over the left, from Aut-Op-Sy, which focuses on the ideas of the Italian anarchist Toni Negri, to Women Leaders Online, for pro-choice Democratic feminists, and carried on intense discussions with people I came to feel I knew in some deep, ultimate way, although I had never met them and didn't want to. What I loved about the Internet was its purity and swiftness, I told him, the feeling of being without a body, of flying into space in all directions at once, of becoming a stream of words going into the blue, a mind touching other minds. I think he took this as a sexual rejection. "You would spend five hours e-mailing with the Women Leaders Online," he said accusingly the day he left, "but you wouldn't spend five hours in bed with me." My women friends all had the same response to this remark: *"Five hours?"*

When he left, I felt like an alcoholic who can finally put the bottle on the table and drink as much as she wants. He wasn't my only target; I Webstalked everyone in his world. His girlfriend, of course, whose prolific output of art journalism I was able to skim online: how apparent, once you looked for them, were the little signs of his growing influence over the past few years—his favorite tag from Nietzsche, a nod to Pierre Bourdieu. I knew what courses she taught and in what month her term on the faculty senate would expire. I followed the fortunes of her books on Amazon, where I did not post nasty anonymous readers' reviews ("Writes like a baton twirler with a Ph.D." —John Ruskin, Yale University; "The worst!" —a reader from Colorado). That would be dishonorable, and, besides, what if she figured out it was me? A search for images turned up three magazine covers, a basket of kittens, and a darkly beautiful, radiantly smiling woman dressed in sequins and lifting a glass of champagne. Fortunately, further research suggested that this was not her but an Italian countess involved in animal rescue. Once, I even tried to listen to a lecture she gave on conceptual art at a remote midwestern university, but I couldn't figure out how to make the audio work, and then suddenly out of the machine a kind of rushing-water sound welled up that could have been hands clapping, and I knew I was on the edge of true self-humiliation and quickly hit Restart, burning with shame.

I Googled his mother, his therapist, his former girl-friends, the members of the Marxist study group we had attended together. I spent a whole night trying to recon-struct, Web site by Web site, what he had told me about a widowed friend: had her husband really been a bigamist, with another wife and child, and did the admiring graduate student who wrote his online obituary know that? My boyfriend had always defended this arrangement, which involved a certain amount of subterfuge: a false phone num-ber and a secret studio reached through a hallway disguised as a closet. That should have told me something. He claimed that the friend—the bigamee?—had had numerous affairs

while her semi-partner or half-husband or whatever you call
him was off with his other family. In fact, he claimed that
she had told him she was unable to be friends with a man
without sleeping with him. You'd never imagine it to meet
her, a shy, trim woman in her seventies with a child's scrubbed
face and the ethereal smile of an ex-nun. That should have
told me something, too.

You think what people say is what matters, an older
friend told me long ago. You think it's all about words. Well,
that's natural, isn't it? I'm a writer; I can float for hours on a
word like "amethyst" or "broom" or the way so many words
sound like what they are: "earth" so firm and basic, "air" so
light, like a breath. You can't imagine them the other way
around: *She plunged her hands into the rich brown air.*
Sometimes I think I would like to be a word—not a big
important word, like "love" or "truth," just a small ordinary
word, like "orange" or "inkstain" or "so," a word that people use so often and so unthinkingly that its specialness has
all been worn away, like the roughness on a pebble in a creek
bed, but that has a solid heft when you pick it up, and if you
hold it to the light at just the right angle you can glimpse
the spark at its core. But of course what my friend meant
was that I ignored inconvenient subtexts, the meaning
behind the meaning: that someone might say he loved you,
but what really mattered was the way he let your hand go
after he said it. It did not occur to me, either, that somebody
might just lie, that there are people who lie for pleasure, for
the feeling of superiority and power. And yet it should have.
When I was a magazine editor, I had an assistant who lied

all the time. Once, on a slow spring day, he called up the NYU Jewish student center, pretended to be a British Jew stranded in New York, and wangled an invitation to its seder. Finally, he went too far, insisting that he had checked the price of a book on Buddhism we had reviewed in the previous issue, and it really was $18.03. "I thought it was odd, too," he mused. "It must be a Zen thing." By the time I worked up the courage to fire him, he had already talked his way into a much better job, and somehow arranged it that his new employers never called me for a reference. Some people just land on their feet.

After the first burst of information, progress was slow. How thrilling was it, really, to discover that his name was mentioned in the abstract of a paper about religious iconography in a particular Catholic girls' school in Western Australia? And yet I kept on. After all, some people, mostly women, not all of them in the porn business, had Web sites hooked up to a camera in their home: you could watch them talking on the phone, eating toast, taking a shower, sleeping, and you could read the diaries in which they nattered on about their day, entries so unenlivened by wit or dash or passion or curiosity that you despaired for the human race. Perhaps if I persisted I would discover, tucked away in a far corner of the Web, a camera recording his new life: Did he and his new girlfriend stay up till three A.M. talking? Did she wake up at night and lie there brimming over with happiness? Of course, a camera couldn't tell you that; all you'd see would be a quilt with a lump under it. Still, I might have watched. It was so terrible to go from living with someone to never seeing him, never even glimpsing the top of his head bent over the art magazines at Barnes & Noble or catching sight of him through the window at the meat counter at Citarella. It was as if he had vanished in a puff of smoke.

Actually, the amazing thing was that, in a way, there was such a camera. Leafing through the *Times* real-estate listings one Sunday, idly looking for that elusive "Classic 6 Riv Vu Needs TLC—Owner Anxious!," I came across an ad for an open house: they were selling her apartment. I wasn't surprised—I had heard they had gotten married. But was I correctly remembering her address? I went to the real estate company's Web site and, sure enough, there was a list of open houses. I clicked on the address I had seen in the paper and up came a floor plan—a typical single-woman one-bedroom, small and boxy, with, I was pleased to note, only one good-sized closet. "Excellent building," chirped the accompanying text. "Great light—sun pours in!" I clicked again and slowly a photograph cranked into focus: the living room. It had obviously been edited and tidied for the buyer's eye, but you could see the inhabitants' taste: spare, contemporary, unencumbered—not his style at all. Still, there was his music stand in the corner; a pillow I had forgotten about was carefully deployed on a gray couch; and there on her wall were the pictures that had formerly hung on my wall—the cat cartoon, the sad trees, the gates of Hell. If only I could enlarge the photo enough times, perhaps I would make out my old spoon and spatula and whisk in the container on the countertop. It was as if the two of them had just left and would come back any minute, laden with groceries, laughing. I clicked on the bedroom photo, but I couldn't make it come up. Perhaps they were in there, basking in the great light.

There wasn't any point going on after that. I had found the magic Web site, the one that was a secret window into reality, but what did it show me that I didn't already know? What difference did it make what color their sofa was? In fact, what had any of my researches revealed that mattered in the end? I had proved to myself that the Internet was indeed a verbal map of the world, the set of propositions that were all that was the case, thrown over the physical world like a medieval rabbi's invisible cloak. But that was all it was. It could mirror facts and events, but not only could it not control or change them, it could not answer my real question: Why? In the months to come, I would look back on this time in my life almost as a kind of out-of-body travel, from which I had returned with nothing but a sense memory of having been somewhere inexpressibly exciting and far away. It wasn't like a dream, exactly, although it had a dream's strange internal logic. It was like looking through the window of an airplane at night, the way the city below appears so near, yet untouchable beyond the glass— a network of lights, flames, stars.

IN THE STUDY
GROUP

TOWARD THE END OF THE 1990S, LONG AFTER MOST people I knew had put their *German Ideology* and their *Eighteenth Brumaire of Louis Napoleon* on the top shelf of the bookcase with the Norton anthology and *Six Greek Plays,* I joined a Marxist study group. This was something I had avoided throughout my twenties and thirties, when Marxism still had some life in it, before it migrated from political economy, the actual subject of Marx's inquiries, to criticism of art and literature, topics about which he had remarkably little to say and where he joined Freud, another big thinker booted out of his original field. The two of them were like heads of bankrupt corporations who had donned blue jeans with elasticized waists and were enjoying a leisurely retirement as film buffs and book clubbers and explorers of trendy new neighborhoods. It was pathetic, really, when you thought about it, the way Marx, that bushy-bearded, carbuncle-tormented Victorian, who had laid bare the secret workings of all human history and caused the foundations of the world to quake, had become just another instant analyst of everything from Hamlet to Batman. Now that Marxism was over, it had a thrift-store charm; you could feel a melancholy curiosity about it, the way you could wonder about a Harris tweed suit, still sporting its Scottish label, that had wound up at the Salvation Army store. How close victory had seemed, and not so long ago! The man I lived with—let's call him G., since that's not his initial—suggested getting some like-minded people together to focus on the anti-Bolshevik tendency of council communism, and I signed on right away. There were about twelve of us, altogether. We met every six weeks or so, in an apartment on Sheridan Square.

To walk into that living room, with its thickly plastered walls and yellowing Braque prints, was to walk into academic bohemia circa 1955. The nubbly brown Danish modern sofas were draped in worn Mexican blankets. A thick shag rug with a bold orange-and-white Scandinavian design lay on the worn wooden floor. The bookshelves were crammed with the paperback classics of my youth: *One-Dimensional Man, Who Rules America?, The Power Elite, No Exit.* The plain, narrow kitchen contained no appliance invented in the last thirty years. I'm making the place sound dusty and shabby, but actually it had an aura of simplicity and good cheer, as if serious, hopeful work was done there, things more important than redecorating and also more conducive to the deeper kinds of happiness. Ruth, to whom the apartment belonged, was an anthropologist who had done significant work on patterns of land tenure in Chiapas. Up there on the eighth floor, with the sun flooding in and a view of clouds and water towers, you could imagine the streets below as they used to be, with bookstores and coffeeshops where the nail salons and Duane Reades are now. It was as if the apartment was part of the alternate version of history council communism itself belonged to—This is what life would look like when the workers ran the show: rumpled and comfortable, with a lot of burnt-sienna accent pillows.

I should say that it was only for me that Marxism seemed over. Surely, I would tell G. at least once a week, it had to count for something that every single self-described Marxist state had turned into an economically backward dictatorship. Irrelevant, he would reply. The real Marxists weren't the Leninists and Stalinists and Maoists—or the Trotskyists either, those bloodthirsty romantics—but libertarian anarchist-socialists, people like Anton Pannekoek, Herman Gorter, Karl Korsch, scholarly believers in true workers' control who had labored in obscurity for most of the twentieth century, enjoyed a late-afternoon moment in the sun after 1968 when they were discovered by the New Left, and had now once again fallen back into the shadows of history, existing mostly as tiny stars in the vast night sky of the Internet, archived on blogs with names like Diary of a Council Communist and Break Their Haughty Power. They were all men. The group itself was mostly men.

This was, as Marxists used to say, no accident. There was something about Marxist theory that just did not appeal to women. G. and I spent a lot of time discussing the possible reasons for this. Was it that women don't allow themselves to engage in abstract speculation, as he thought? That Marxism is incompatible with feminism, as I sometimes suspected? Or perhaps the problem was not Marxism but Marxists: in its heyday men had kept a lock on it as they did on everything they considered important; now, in its decline, Marxism had become one of those obsessive lonely-guy hobbies, like collecting stamps or 78s. Maybe, like collecting, it was related, through subterranean psychological pathways, to sexual perversions, most of which seemed to be male as well. You never hear about a female foot fetishist, or a woman like the high-school history teacher of a friend of mine who kept dated bottles of his own urine on a closet shelf. Perhaps women's need for speculation is satisfied by the intense curiosity they bring to daily life, the way their collecting masquerades as fashion and domesticity—instead of old records, shoes and ceramic mixing bowls—and their perversity can be satisfied simply by enacting the highly artificial role of Woman, by becoming, as it were, fetishizers of their own feet.

Our study group, then, was typical in that it was mostly men, and it was also typical in that one of those men—G.— was, despite much egalitarian rhetoric, the leader, the one who sat in the big rocking chair and framed and paced the discussion. The group was unusual, though, in that a number of the men actually had working-class jobs. True, G.

taught philosophy and Richard was a musicologist and Miguel was getting a Ph.D. in economics; Neil was a child psychologist and his wife, Jenny, was a computer programmer; beautiful zaftig Samira from Lebanon worked for a foundation. But Quentin, who did outreach with homeless drug addicts and on bad days looked as if he might have been one himself, was so poor he read his e-mail at the library. Patrick was a firefighter; Matt was a carpenter; Len drove a truck. André, who lived just outside Paris, where he wrote witty, urgent articles for *Les temps modernes* under a pseudonym, was an electrician.

Except for Matt, who had dropped out of grad school, they were self-educated: working-class intellectuals straight out of the nineteenth century. They came home after work, changed into clean clothes, and began their other life, of reading, writing, talking, and, in the case of Matt, smoking phenomenal amounts of pot—what the working class might have been, minus the pot, but for the invention of television. They knew an astonishing amount about a wide variety of subjects; they had read everything. The women in the group were mostly girlfriends. In fact, although I didn't know this at the time, several were, or had been, the girlfriends of my boyfriend. He liked to keep them around. The style of the men was the one that always at first makes my heart beat faster and then sink into lethargy and resentment: intellectual self-display. Matt, in particular, went in for long, ecstatic arias. "Every day," he would say, his long, thin, angular body wreathed in bluish cigarette smoke that made him look like a very cool DJ or possibly Satan as imagined by Paul Auster, "working people get up and make the world. Every *day*. They keep the factories going, they run the subways and drive the trucks, they put up buildings, they fix whatever is broken, they plant and grow and harvest and make the food, they press the buttons on the elevators that take the CEOs to their offices on the fortieth floor! Where those CEOs do *nothing*." At this point the group would perk up at what was indeed an amazing thought: What if, one day, the workers simply decided not to go to work? Our world, so thick and solid, with its factories, prisons, highways, schools, vast construction projects of every kind, its dense, sticky web of social and economic hierarchies, rested in the end on Will: the willingness of the oppressed to perpetuate it, when they could blow it away with a single collective breath. It followed that when the capitalist system collapsed, under circumstances that were impossible to foretell and pointless even to speculate about, the workers would know what to do. They wouldn't need a vanguard party or a group of intellectuals to tell them how to run the world; they were already doing it. They would organize themselves—exactly how and for what no one could predict, but it would be wonderful. Matt would get all excited imagining how instead of remodeling lofts in Tribeca for recording-industry hotshots, he could use the same skills to fix up apartments in Bedford-Stuyvesant.

This was the part I could never understand. If one couldn't predict or shape or control or cause the end of capitalism, if whatever ideas we had about it would all be swept away in the great deluge that was to come, if intellectuals would be in any case irrelevant and the working class would spontaneously take charge of production, what was the point of flogging ourselves through all this strenuous reading? Why discuss and debate when we could just wait and see? It was all very well to say that activism and community organizing and electoral politics were pointless—the futility of such endeavors was a given to G. and Matt, the subject of considerable sarcastic eye-rolling—but so, by the same argument, was being in a study group. Surely voting couldn't be a *more* ineffectual way to shape the future than talking to each other in Ruth's living room? "We're intellectuals," G. would say with a shrug when I raised this point. "So we try to understand things. Even if it's useless." But had not Marx himself written, in the eleventh thesis on Feuerbach, "Up until now philosophers have only interpreted the world in various ways. The point, however, is to change it"? How did my reading Guy Debord's *Society of the Spectacle* help me change the world? Well, actually, I only skimmed it.

The meetings began around ten, with bagels, orange juice, and coffee, and went on all day. All day! The glare bouncing off the high, wide windows, the smoke from Jeff's cigarettes, the endless drone of male voices made the sessions simultaneously intense and soporific, like the reading itself, which I had usually not finished and sometimes barely begun. That was my useless teenagerish rebellion, the flip side of my hero worship of G. that was so puzzling to my friends. How could they not see what made him stand out? He was so clever, so dashing, so handsome. "You should go out with that tall guy in the overcoat," my husband told me over drinks while the lawyers bickered over our divorce, and indeed that coat was a splendid garment, romantically long and threadbare. Walter Benjamin might have worn it escaping from Berlin. My heart melted when G. took up a collection from the group for the train fares of Patrick who came from Boston, and Quentin, from Baltimore. It was the sort of thoughtful gesture, redolent of left solidarity and shared privation, that I imagined only he would think of. In his old-fashioned herringbone jackets and rimless glasses, G. seemed to incarnate an entire alternate history of the Left, a Left with no gulags or murdered poets or nutty agricultural ideas. Its touchstones were the Paris Commune, Rosa Luxemburg and Karl Liebknecht, the German workers' councils, the anarchists in Spain. Failures all, and finished long ago. Perhaps, I sometimes thought, council communism was so appealing precisely because it had had so little chance to be dirtied by the world.

Perhaps, too, even studying council communism was a way of not facing obvious truths about people—their selfishness and power seeking, their capacity for self-delusion and delight in screwing each other over. It wasn't as if the group members were so pure. Consider the case of Billy. This was Matt's friend and fellow grad school dropout, as plump and pale and quiet as a mushroom, who had come to the group in the beginning but was now living in obscurity upstate and working off the books to avoid having to pay child support. According to Matt, Billy was the victim of his evil girlfriend, who had used him to get pregnant after he'd rescued her from the insane asylum and who was now trying to extract cash from him for the baby he had never wanted. "Wait," I would say. "He took her out of a mental hospital? He relied on a crazy woman to take charge of birth control? Like it would kill him to use a condom! Somebody's got to support that baby—why not Billy?" This would invariably provoke sardonic remarks about family values and welfare reform and the folly of expecting a sad sack like Billy to assume any kind of responsibility, even over his own penis. Conversations like this made me hate men. What if socialism—all that warmhearted folderol about community and solidarity and sharing—was just an elaborate con job, a way for men to avoid supporting their kids? I wouldn't put it past them—I had always felt that left-wing men were the worst. In college I would look around the cafeteria tables where the anti-war activists sat for hours over tuna melts and Cokes and think how sad it was that my politics had led me to this very small pool of potential boyfriends, all seriously problematic. The Maoists of the Progressive Labor Party were rigid and bizarre and always trying to get you to hand out leaflets at six in the morning. The rock-and-rollers and Weatherman sympathizers were callow and conceited and usually stoned. And yet it was not possible to be with a man who was conservative or apolitical, or even just a Democrat, someone who might have, say, voted for Hubert Humphrey. Even a McCarthy supporter was pushing it. Those people were so naïve.

~

A curious feature of the group was that although G. was the de facto leader, only some of the members shared his politics, or even understood what they were. Judith, G.'s secret girlfriend, was a liberal feminist whose academic field was Victorian fiction. When I asked G. why she was suddenly interested in plunging into abstruse Marxist theory, he said she was looking for a challenge to take her mind off her divorce. It seemed to be working—she looked quite radiant listening to G. explain the declining rate of profit. Ruth and Samira were "progressives," and didn't seem to notice that the men in the group never uttered this word without scorn. They were always signing petitions and going to demonstrations and writing letters to their congresspeople about FCC regulations or the minimum wage, activities the men regarded as not only futile but undignified, a bending of the knee to power. Quentin, the Baltimore poverty worker, was hot for grassroots action. He self-published a newsletter that was mostly a list of all the wildcat strikes going on around the world. There were always more of these than you might think, especially if you overlooked the size of the world.

Len was even worse—he actually tried to organize his fellow Teamsters into supporting a dissident faction in the union, in open disregard of G.'s belief that unions were the way workers were co-opted and managed on behalf of capital. But Len was a special case—he was still extracting himself from his intense involvement in News and Letters, a sect famous for its stern but shifting line and uranium-like propensity for fission. The group's members' chief activity, besides discovering and ousting heretics from their midst, was reading Hegel. Those who survived the double barrage of show trials and German philosophy were iron men of dispute, hairsplitters without equal. For having the wrong view of the breakup of Yugoslavia they had called Len out on the carpet and strongly encouraged him to study Hegel's *Phenomenology of Spirit* before he got any more bright ideas, and such was their psychological power that he carried Hegel everywhere, like a lunchbox. Two News and Letters members showed up at one meeting, ostensibly to join in the discussion but really, we all believed, to keep tabs on Len—Victor and Joan, a tall, thin, pallid married couple, with glasses and discolored cannibal teeth, who looked as if they spent their days writing pamphlets in damp basements, like the anarchists in *The Secret Agent.* Within minutes, I was arguing with Joan about Kosovar independence, even as I thought, How strange, none of us knows anything about it! There was something about them that provoked you to disagree, the way pepper makes you want to sneeze.

Len stayed. Quentin disappeared, and sent Ruth a letter excoriating the group for its do-nothing philosophy. "He wants to be the Big Activist Leader," G. said, mockingly—the same thing he told me when André, in town on a visit, reported on his work organizing the huge marches and rallies of the unemployed that galvanized France that year. Samira left, too, for a while—she was spending weekends with a playwright she'd met on the Internet—and then one day she was back, pale and thin and more beautiful than ever. Matt turned forty, quit smoking, and became a health nut. He gave up meat, and then real food entirely. He sat through the festive dinner parties that ended the meetings, sipping Gary Null's Green Stuff out of a thermos. He drank so much carrot juice that his skin took on a faint orange sheen. He claimed his regimen was causing hair to sprout on his receding hairline, and sometimes it did seem as if a soft, colorless fuzz was blooming there.

~

Why did I stay? When I skipped a meeting, I could feel G.'s disapproval. But there was more to it than that. The group offered me a way to rethink my own increasingly marginal, futile-seeming, dated liberal pinkishness. Once at a demonstration I saw a well-known woman writer, short and stout, with snapping bright brown eyes and flyaway gray hair, in a long black skirt and a Mexican peasant blouse. She was turning a paper roller like the street singer's prop in *The Threepenny Opera*, on which the sins of the Reagan administration were illustrated with stick figures, and she explicated them in a singsong parody-kindergarten-teacher voice: *Ooh, look! Less money for children, more money for war!* That's my future, I thought, that will be me: I will be a well-meaning folk-art-decorated person who embarrasses herself for worthy causes. I wanted a radical critique—there had to be more to the Left than calling for more funds for Head Start. The problem was, a truly radical critique, a perspective that got high enough off the ground to see the pattern whole—how the very institutions that seem to challenge the system, like unions or left-wing parties or nonprofits, are in fact part of it—left one with nothing to do except read and theorize. "You wait," G. would say when I got excited about some new thing—the U.S. Labor Party or John Sweeney's attempts to revitalize the AFL-CIO, or even the Million Mom March. "In two years, nobody will even be talking about this." The fact is, he was usually right.

At one level the group appealed because, unlike most of the Left, its politics weren't about liberal guilt. They were too abstract for that. You didn't have to feel bad because you weren't giving all your money to the homeless. The homeless would have to save themselves. "Beat the poor!" G. would say, quoting Baudelaire, meaning, The workers will have to suffer till they give up their illusions. In a way it was the Left's version of Republicanism: if you're a victim, it's your own fault. Actually, though, I didn't get rid of my liberal guilt; I still raised money for Afghan women and bought overpriced Mars bars from black teenagers on the subway. I simply acquired a new guilt: the feeling that I should like and admire the other group members and didn't because I was a snob. Why couldn't I take Len seriously, when he was obviously a good and kind person who worked harder in a day than I did in a month? Why did Matt's perorations make me feel like I was on a bad date, where the man talks endlessly about himself? Why, when I saw G. surrounded by this pickup team of acolytes, did I feel pity—a pity I immediately suppressed and replaced with self-reproach for judging him by bourgeois standards of "success"? Once I skipped the afternoon session to have coffee uptown with two old friends I hadn't seen in ages. The cozy little restaurant with its steamed-over windows and well-dressed women sharing elegant desserts might as well have been on Saturn. They must think I'm insane, I thought as I chirped away brightly about the all-day meetings, the readings, about Matt and Len and my brilliant underappreciated boyfriend. I sound like I'm in a cult.

It was only after G. moved out and I stopped going to the meetings that I realized how true that was. I had been, in a way, in a cult. Like all cults, the group was organized around a charismatic leader, G. It had a secret sexual agenda, which was for him to gather his current and former girlfriends together, and it had a secret revelation, a way of understanding the world that made sense only when you got deep inside it and then, as if a lightbulb suddenly switched on, seemed to illuminate everything. Perhaps it was not very likely that current trends in occupational health and mortality had been completely explained in 1975 by a graduate student G. had known in Cambridge, who, after producing his one article, published in a tiny left-wing journal, had faded from view. But it was possible—if you squinted at reality at just the right angle you could see it.

That was the dark side—the rivalries and sexual undercurrents, the fetish of the arcane, the political passivity that coexisted strangely with a belief that something terribly important and real, something we called "politics," was taking place right there in Ruth's living room. In a way we missed the whole point of council communism, which was collective self-reliance and egalitarianism and the constant renewal of energy through engagement with concrete reality. We were like the German proletariat, which rose up, forced out the Kaiser, ended the First World War, and then turned in its weapons because it trusted the perfidious socialists. Well, you can see why: nobody likes going to meetings all the time. But perhaps that was another problem with council communism: it relied too much on people being alert and rational and not having hidden motives—motives hidden even from themselves.

~

Those dark parts aren't the whole story, though. There were good things too. Unlike most of the academics and writers I've known, for example, the people in the group seemed genuinely interested in each other's ideas. When Patrick, our firefighter, read out loud one of his meticulously detailed, erudite essays about neocapitalism in China or the prospect for workers' resistance in Vietnamese garment factories, everyone leaned forward with anticipation. Now we were going to learn something. Now we were in for a treat! Was that only because nothing tangible, money or fame or careers, was at stake? There were moments when, through the blue haze of Matt's cigarettes, I could glimpse what thinking together might be, something joyful and devoted. Thinking together was not something I was good at or, to be honest, cared to be good at. But maybe that was my own limitation. Some of the people in the group were a little odd, perhaps, but then so are most people. If you accept the world as it is, though, if you are strange the way everyone else is strange, people don't look at you closely or inquire about your motives the way they do of those with different ideas. You're like one of those quiet people whom the neighbors can't believe ax-murdered his whole family, because he smiled in the elevator and said, Yes, it looks like rain. In the same way, it's easy to make fun of council communism as impractical and unrealistic. Of course it was unrealistic!— to imagine that the working class could run a whole complex modern society by organizing and linking democratic and egalitarian governing groups in workplaces. To insist that the society's scut work be shared, so that nobody got stuck for life cleaning toilets or glaring from behind the counter at the Department of Motor Vehicles. To ask how scarce luxury goods, like grand cru Burgundy or opera tickets, could be distributed in a way that didn't reflect and entrench privilege. G. used to infuriate me when he suggested that under communism everyone would change their work every few years; he insisted that, with exceptions like science or medicine, anyone could pick up the skills needed for any job in a couple of weeks. Wow, I'd say, I hope I'm not on I-95 when you come barrelling down in a semi. He made communism sound like one of those vocational schools advertised on the covers of matchbooks. But were these woolly utopian proposals wilder than the accepted wisdom of the 1990s—for example, that immense wealth could be generated and the economy transformed by Internet start-ups that produced and sold nothing, that "the market" was the ultimate arbiter of every question, and that every human need or desire could be met by the quest for profit?

∼

The truth is, I miss the group. Sometimes when I walk past Ruth's building I look up and see the lights burning in her living room window. I imagine them all up there, talking away seriously and purposefully, leafing through books and reading passages out loud. There's a fresh pot of coffee on the table, and many copies of *The New York Times* lie spread out and scattered on the floor. Matt tells a long story. Samira passes around a petition and everyone signs. If I were there I would be fidgety and irritable, as at a family gathering that has gone on too long, but since I am down on the street I forget that part. I even forget that the reason I am not up there with the others is that I could not stand to be in the same room as G. for even two seconds. Instead I find myself wondering if Len is still wrestling with Hegel, and if he agrees with him that the owl of Minerva takes flight when night is falling, that a historical era can be grasped only when it is over, that you understand something only when it is too late to do anything about it.

Long after I left the group, I finally read the seminal text of anti-Bolshevik communism, *Workers' Councils*, by Anton Pannekoek. The writing, as I'd feared, was dense and flat and full of technical terminology, although not without flashes of wit, and the translation had not quite made it all the way from Dutch into English. Still, the more I read the more I felt that here was something wonderful and noble. Even the section headings moved me: "The Task," "The Fight," "The Foe," "The War," "The Peace." Who writes like that today? Who thinks like that today? Those confident monosyllables seemed to speak of a whole world of lost assumptions: that truth existed and was knowable, that human beings could consciously shape history and determine their fate, that this is our work, together and alone.

I thought of Pannekoek, who was not only a Marxist theorist but a notable astronomer—the astronomical institute of the University of Amsterdam is named after him—living alone and writing his steadfast and hopeful book day by day while the Second World War raged on, while the Nazis occupied Holland, and Anne Frank and her family were rounded up with the other Jews, and people starved in the streets in the terrible winter of 1944. It would have been easy then to believe that civilization was finished, that human beings were wolves—no, worse than wolves. Perhaps, even though he was a scientist, Pannekoek looked up at the stars and wondered if they sparkled with malice. But he kept writing—what else could he do, at that point?—and little by little the pages piled up on his desk. Then one day the war was over, and he put down his pen and looked around him and thought, And so we begin. Again.

SISTERHOOD

OSTOYEVSKY SAYS SOMEWHERE THAT WE ATTRACT to ourselves events that are like ourselves. If so, it must also be true that people who experience the same things are in some way like each other. After G. left and I found out about his other women, this thought disturbed me deeply. Because what if the kind of person your life says you most resemble is precisely the kind of person—the kind of woman—you most don't want to be?

"He told me he could be himself sexually with me as with no one else," Judith said, in that offhand, take-it-or-leave-it way of hers, as if only stating the obvious. We were sitting in her little studio off Riverside Drive, late at night at the end of August, a few days after G. decamped, having it out. I had heard a bit from him about this apartment—

how she had had to move from a two-bedroom when the rent went up, after losing the big co-op in which she had raised her children when her ex-husband stiffed her in the divorce. Judith and G. were colleagues, and her travails had been the subject of endless conversation between him and me—her ex-husband's ingenious methods of avoiding child support, her many awful boyfriends, the many extra jobs she took to make ends meet. Her life was rich with comic scandal, like the time her husband's girlfriend assumed her identity to use the family health insurance and Judith got the bills, and the time her big-shot-academic boyfriend told her how lucky he felt to have women for all his needs—his wife for domestic comfort, his longtime mistress in Boston for "spiritual communion," and Judith for sex. I knew this man's writing too—in my "pro-life hypocrisy" file I'd saved an essay in which he'd urged accidentally pregnant teenagers to be open to the glorious unpredictability of life. What made these stories funny was that none of Judith's tormentors felt they were doing anything wrong. The girl-friend didn't have her own insurance, so what was she supposed to do? But under the comic routines, Judith's life had the inevitably downward plot of a novel by Zola, a long, slow slide from prosperity as a married mother of three to scrimping along in a single room and feeling lucky because it was a pretty room, with lots of light and an oval of plaster roses on the ceiling, and at least she hadn't had to move to Brooklyn yet.

She told me she had been sleeping with G. virtually the entire time I had known him, at the office and at her house but not my house, that he always said he didn't love her, that he put her down and was cruel to her but was also her best friend, that she had wept in the street when she glimpsed us at breakfast through the window of a local diner, and that she had no sexual inhibitions at all. Now that she mentioned it, I remembered that long ago he had called her the sex goddess of the Upper West Side, but I had always assumed that was a joke: she was older than me, and while not unattractive, she gave the impression of someone struggling gamely but unsuccessfully against bitterness and gloom. From time to time as we talked she would pull down a marbled composition book—she had kept a diary ever since she was a teenager, she explained—and hunt for an entry to refresh her memory or demonstrate that she was telling the truth. She wanted me to understand that she, not he, had ended their affair a few months before. "Let's see, where is that passage?" she muttered, flicking through pages of black, urgent handwriting. "Here: 'June 9th. Broke it off with G. I feel sad but it had to be done.' Voilà." She looked up with the satisfaction of someone who's won a bet about who said "My country, right or wrong" or "I shall return."

"It sounds as if he didn't love me, really," I said as I stood up to go. "That he just lived with me all those years out of convenience." "Oh no, I'm sure he loved you," she said soothingly. "Or at least if he didn't, he repressed it." Like everyone in this story, Judith had spent years in therapy and knew her Freud.

You would think I would hate her, but what was the point? Both of us, after all, had been rejected for someone else—*another* other woman. I had always enjoyed Judith's scrappy, wisecracking manner and been happy to see her. She had been to my house for Thanksgiving and had come to my book party. Once when we had an extra ticket, we took her to the theater with my father. And now we had so much in common! For months, we e-mailed each other almost every day. I would come home from running errands and rush to the computer still wearing my jacket and scarf. When her name popped up in the in-box I was as excited as if hearing from a lover. What, he really *said* that to you? He did *what?* You are a good person who deserves happiness, we told each other over and over, attractive, kind, loving, generous, forgiving; the problem is, men are rats. Again and again we enumerated their faults: the way they compartmentalized their lives and feelings, and played women off against each other, and felt so entitled, and were so cold and heartless. At the same time as she scorned sexual fidelity as bourgeois and naïve, Judith valued her capacity for what she called "attachment." She was even attached to me. "Sometimes I see the three of us ending up together," she wrote, "in wheelchairs in the same old-age home." She seemed to find that a cheerful prospect. Yet Judith's talent for bonding was a quality man after man had failed to appreciate. They took what they wanted and moved on. I had had this conversation before, of course—in a way I had been having it all my life: Why don't they love us the way we love them? How could they ignore, forget, dismiss, neglect, not pay attention, not care, say this and then do that? But I had never before had it with a woman who accused of insufficient sensitivity to herself by the man who was, after all, living with me.

It was bound to end badly. One night I woke up suddenly in bed, like William Hurt in his prison cell at the end of *Body Heat*, when it comes to him in a flash how Kathleen Turner had double-crossed him. I saw Judith and G. laughing and bustling around the stove, a few months before he left; they were making paella for our Marxist study group. She had brought her own special pan and her own special recipe. Not only had she invited herself to Thanksgiving and come to my book party and accepted an invitation to the theater *with my father*, I fumed, she had made herself at home *in my kitchen!* Not that I ever used it much, but still. The whole evening came back to me: I had drunk wine in the living room with the rest of the group while the two of them crashed about gaily among the cabinets, bustling and laughing and calling each other "Professor," and I had felt like I was swimming underwater in a glass box.

I wrote to Judith breaking off communications, and she promptly e-mailed back that she had been about to do the same; her friends and therapist all thought she was crazy to have anything to do with me. They had a point: I could have forwarded her e-mails around the globe. But why would I do that? Information was what I wanted from her: the underside of the carpet I thought I had been standing on. I hadn't exactly pretended friendship to get her to talk, as she accused me of doing, but I had indeed been interviewing her, quietly and methodically, like a journalist gathering facts for a story called "How I Could Have Been So Stupid."

I asked leading questions, I phrased things different ways, I bit my tongue. Once I had extracted from her everything she was willing to tell me and more, I either (self-exculpating version) allowed myself to feel the true scope of my wrath or (not-so-virtuous version) treated her the way Janet Malcolm says reporters always treat their sources: I betrayed her.

Judith wasn't the only other woman I got in touch with. Erica, a sweet, rather fey art historian, talked to me on the phone for hours. Her relationship with G. had mostly been by telephone too, back when he was living with the woman before me. It was one of those intense flirtations that have all the ups and downs and close calls and anxieties of a love affair. Instead of sex, it revolved around contact lenses; she lived in Maine and he used to send her a special kind available only in New York. One night he had called her from a phone booth on the street. I knew that phone booth, at the end of his old street in the Village—this was back in the days before cell phones, when people had to slip out of the house to call their secret love interests. Immediately I pictured the scene: early spring, night, mist, branches making lacy shadows under the streetlights. After a few minutes of romantic banter, she heard a gruff man's voice saying, *Hey, buddy, you gonna be much longer? You been on that phone for an hour and a half!* "He must have been going down a list," Erica said, "and finally he got to me." She blew up at him, and it was years before he called again.

And then there was Judith's friend Liz. She taught linguistics in the Midwest and had actually stopped coming to

New York to see him when he moved in with me. "I don't think there was anything wrong with us for falling for him," she wrote. "I just happened to meet him at a susceptible moment. It was like catching a cold because you're tired and run-down." Some cold. Ten years later, she was still alone. In our e-mails, we mostly focused on contrasting our resolve and self-respect with Judith's weakness and abjection: imagine, she was still obsessing over their every encounter in the hallway at the wretched university where they both taught, turning over every word in search of that tiny gold spangle of hope! Not. Like. Us. Liz suggested I write G. an apologetic letter taking entire responsibility for the failure of our relationship. She was sure this would have him camping on my doorstep within minutes. She offered this advice not because she believed I was at fault, although of course I partly was, one always is, but because years of therapy had led her to believe that the best way of dealing with men like G. was to agree with them completely while maintaining secret reservations and provisos, sort of like the Yalta agreement. Yes, she admitted, this practice might look masochistic, but it was actually a subtle interior triumph over your own vulnerability to sadism. You freely give them what they want and so prove to yourself that they can't *make* you give them what they want. But to them it looks exactly the same! I said, The effect is the same! Yes, she agreed, but that only shows how insensitive men are.

There were other women too, whom I met around town. A famous philosopher, a beautiful Polish dissident, a pair of anthropologists, a trio of painters. At one dinner party I realized three out of the five women there had been his girl-friends back in the early 1980s. We eyed one another slyly over the roast lamb and braised cauliflower as if to say, Let's talk. After I published the essay "Learning to Drive," I got letters: I think I knew the man you are writing about in grad-uate school. . . . I dated him in the sixties. . . . He said I was too consumerist and didn't care about the working class. . . . Who's that young woman you said he was involved with? . . . Would it be possible to send me a recent photo? I rummaged in my picture drawer and found two; I passed up the one in which he looked liked a lofty scholar deep in contemplation and sent her the one that made him look like a chipmunk.

I had thought of G. as a kind of Don Giovanni, but I began to see that this wasn't quite right. The Don had been indiscriminate; women were all the same to him. All he cared about were conquest and novelty, adding names to his list. But G. had a type. The women he went for were not especially beautiful and not especially young. But they were all artists, writers, academics: smart, serious, romantic. There was an essential solitude about them, as if deep inside they were still twelve years old, reading *Wuthering Heights* under the blankets with a flashlight. Even if they were over forty, married, with three teenage kids and a Ph.D., like Judith, or dashed from conference to conference like the famous philosopher, there was a part of them—some shy, neglected princess pacing in her tower—that was still wait-ing for life to begin. I had been a bit like that when I'd met him, and maybe the new young one was too, a daydreamer, a late bloomer, hot for intensity, passion, *it*. As I pieced events together, she had waited for him a long time, and that must have been hard to do. After all, I thought of her as a "younger woman," but she was only young compared to him.

Naturally, they, she—we—were feminists. The last sort of woman who would expect herself to fall for a philanderer in a panama hat. A panama hat! Get real. "The first time I met him," Liz wrote, "I thought he was affected, sexist and bizarre. That old-fashioned suit, the way he bowed over my hand as if he was going to kiss it. Then I met him again and *boom*." I hadn't even needed that second time. All he had had to do was introduce himself, and half an hour later I was making my way home through the damp gray streets, on fire: I was like a flame in fog. My friends didn't like him; my therapist was suspicious. "He sounds like a charming bounder," said Dr. Bone, but all I took away from that remarkably astute observation was the delicious Victorian turn of phrase, so unexpected in cautious Dr. B. I didn't care what he thought. After all, when I wasn't mooning over G., I was patiently explaining to Dr. Bone, at the cost of three dollars a minute plus taxi fare, that psychiatry was a male plot aimed at keeping women docile and domestic. "Some feminists would say," he countered mildly, "that romantic love is a male plot too. The velvet glove on the iron fist." "Oh well," G. laughed when I repeated that. "An iron fist in a velvet glove is better than an iron fist."

～

Feminism was supposed to be about the things women had in common, and I had always thought of myself as someone who liked women. When someone—usually a woman; in fact, always a woman—said I "thought like a man" I felt insulted both for women and myself; it was as if I was being expelled from the tribe. I love, for example, the instant intimacy women can have with each other, how within minutes of meeting you find yourself sharing life stories, like characters in Russian novels but certainly not like American men. Like Judith's misadventures, the stories women tell each other about themselves emphasize the comical, the improbable, the vaguely malevolent but always entertaining twists and turns of fate, with the speaker shaking her head in wonder as if she were a passive audience at the movie of her life, and every story has the same shrug of a punch line: *What can you do?* Now I saw slapped down on the table what women really shared: the longing for male approval, the bartering of self-respect for relationship, the endless making of excuses, the obstinate refusal to know what you know. How exasperated I had been by these very qualities, by women who excused their husbands' hostile digs and putdowns as "just his sense of humor," who read threats and explosiveness as proof of love, who wouldn't stand up for themselves and spent immense amounts of mental energy denying to themselves that that's what they were doing. All my adult life I had wanted to rescue women—but I had also felt superior to the ones I tried to help and was annoyed when they didn't take my excellent advice: don't waste your fertile years on that married man, find a sitter, finish your degree, get a lawyer, get a *better* lawyer. Look, see, face facts. But what about the facts—encyclopedias of facts—that I had brushed aside because, like Judith, Erica, Liz, and all those other women, I wanted what I wanted? I had not taken my own advice either. The truth was, I was just another woman. I was just like them.

～

"Maybe I'm not cut out for monogamy," G. had said to me early on. "Maybe I should just live in a room by myself and have girlfriends." Another woman might have said, "Now, where did I put my coat?" Being a madly infatuated rationalist who had read her Simone de Beauvoir, I took a deep breath and carefully and calmly explained that of course he had to make up his own mind about how he wanted to live, and that I understood fidelity wasn't for everyone, that some people could be perfectly happy without it, but I wanted to give my whole self in love and I couldn't do that if I was being compared to other women on a daily basis (which I was) or if our relationship was only tentative and provisional (which it was). "Sweetie!" he said when I finished. "I love it that you can say how you feel without getting angry at me." That other woman would have slammed the door behind her before he'd finished speaking.

They say philanderers are attractive to women because of the thrill of the chase—you want to be the one to capture and tame that wild quarry. But what if a deeper truth is that women fall for such men because they want to *be* those men? Autonomous, in charge, making their own rules. Imagine that room G. spoke of, in which the women would come and go—is there not something attractive about it?

Rain tapping softly on the tin ceiling, a desk, a lamp, a bed. A woman dashes up the narrow stairs, her raincoat flaring, her wet face lifted up like a flower. And then, the next day— maybe even the same day—different footsteps, another expectant face. I had to admit, it was an exciting scenario. You wouldn't want to be one of the women trooping up and down the staircase, but you might want to be the man who lived in the room.

~

Perhaps, if a woman really could choose, she would not be so kind or considerate or high-minded after all, or so inter- ested in all that soft, damp, pleading "attachment" either. Wasn't that what men had feared about feminism back in the 1960s, that women would start picking and choosing and judging and dropping, serving themselves, the way men always had? Perhaps the way women think about love is part of that slave religion Nietzsche talks about, a mystification of powerlessness. Perhaps women cast a spell on themselves in order to cast a spell on men, a leftover from the days when you needed a man to survive; but of course you couldn't put it like that, even to yourself, much less to him, or the spell wouldn't work. Maybe romance really is the velvet glove on the iron fist and Utopia would be everyone living in their room, and visiting the rooms of others. Maybe, in the future, when women's psychology catches up to their mate- rial circumstances, we'll live in sugar-cube cities made up entirely of studio apartments. I could hardly say that I found domesticity erotic, once I got over the sheer miracle of having the beloved right there, to be touched and looked at and talked with whenever I wanted. I would have been a good girlfriend for a political prisoner, writing long letters and living in a fever of anticipation—*just think, darling, only fifteen more years!*—and having the intoxication of romantic love without the loss of self it seemed to entail.

What would the world be like if women stopped being women—shut the tea-and-sympathy shop, closed down the love store, gave up the slave religion? Could the world go on without romantic love, all iron fist, no velvet glove? The Germans thought Nietzsche was great, and look what it got them. And yet, in the end, nobody loves a victim, even—especially—the other victims. "Down among the women," as Fay Weldon wrote, back when she still was one. "What a place to be!" Now she writes books telling women to fake orgasms because nature has designed them to hardly ever have them and why make a man feel bad about something that isn't his fault? In other words, practice the slave religion; just don't believe in it yourself. But why would anyone do that if they can buy their own shoes?

～

Years ago I found a pair of Japanese prints in an antiques shop in Maine. The first showed a knight on horseback with a pair of attendants on foot; one holds his furled standard, the other his sword. They are wading across a shallow river in a beautiful celadon-green landscape, and give off an air of dignity and confidence. In the second, a beautiful woman is wandering through a similar landscape, only it's raining and the wind is blowing her kimono about; she has no horse, no weapon, no flag; an elderly maidservant struggles to keep a paper umbrella over her mistress's head. This is what happens when a woman goes out into the world alone, those pictures say; his adventure is her misfortune. The hell with that, I thought. I bought the man's picture and left the forlorn beauty behind to fend for herself, even though I felt sorry for her and as if I was betraying my sex. I wish I could have given her a horse and a sword and a copy of *The Feminine Mystique*. But the truth was, I didn't want her over my desk, wringing her hands and weeping. I wanted to be that bold, well-girded knight. Or at least to look at him.

~

G. had a term for women who had slept with the same man. "Think of them as your sperm sisters," he would say cheerfully when I looked glum at the mention of previous girlfriends. I would try to see myself bobbing playfully in the dark blue sea, sleek and happy, one in a herd of seals or a pod of whales, buoyant with female solidarity and many layers of fat. I had forgotten that I had ever met Erica or Liz in the nonvirtual world, but eventually an old memory swam up: Judith, Erica, Liz, G. and I in an Italianate garden in Santa Barbara, where G. had brought me along to an academic conference soon after I'd left my husband. I had felt sad and tense, disregarded, without being able to explain why—did I simply always need to be the center of attention? The next day Erica and I walked into town and found ourselves browsing in a jewelry supply store, a long, dark room where glass beads flashed in hundreds of tiny drawers like the treasure in those miniature pirate chests people put in their aquariums. "You look so much alike," the proprietress exclaimed, although I saw nothing of myself in Erica's gentle dreaminess, her ripply blond mermaid hair. "Are you sisters?"

To be the pasha, surrounded by his harem—it's the oldest male fantasy in the book. And you would be surprised— I was surprised—by how many feminists buy into a kind of women's mirror-image version: jealousy or possessiveness as a patriarchal holdover that divides women from one another, polygamy as a form of female cooperation, a kind of wifely labor union that keeps the man in line: *Tough luck, boss, it's mac and cheese for supper again and young Fatima's got exams tomorrow, so you'll have to make do with me.* In some feminist circles, criticizing polygamy—polygyny, actually, because it only goes one way—is a good way to be accused of cultural chauvinism, but the harem isn't just for Muslims or old-school Mormons. Lifetime TV is always running movies in which the ex-wife and the new wife bond. True, usually for that to happen the first wife has to be stricken with a fatal disease, albeit one that leaves her beautiful and smiling and clearly still Susan Sarandon.

"The only thing I didn't like in your story was the way you went after that other woman, the friend," one feminist historian said to me, after "Learning to Drive" came out. It would be easy to say that as a single woman she had a vested interest in the claims of "friends." But I could see what she meant. It wasn't that I had no right to be angry at Judith (*with my father! in my kitchen!*). But she wasn't the one who'd said to me *love, adore, deep, stay, always.* He had said those words. And although he hadn't said those exact words to her, maybe he'd said the ones next door—*need, pleasure, here, yes, now*—the ones that can make you think that those other words are just about to come, and if you're not careful you can look around and realize it's been, what, fifteen years.

~

Liz published an article in an academic quarterly describing G. as a genius and his new book as a major contribution to its field. Erica sank out of sight. The Polish exile took up with a married man. One painter became more famous, the others more obscure. The anthropologists continued to puzzle over their clans and tribes. I met the famous philosopher at a party and she told me that she had never had with him the intensely sexual affair he had told me had taken him years to get over. She would never have done anything to jeopardize her marriage, she said; mostly they'd just talked. I glimpse Judith every now and then around the neighborhood, darting into the subway at 103rd Street or browsing among the tables of cut-rate underwear and African knickknacks at a street fair. Maybe she has a new man in her life, someone honorable and kind. Or maybe that's all over for her now, and she goes home and sits by the window of her one room that had been some bustling nineteenth-century family's parlor, writing in her diary and remembering how long ago she had looked out a different window and thought, *Everything is about to change. Everything!*

She looks older, younger, exactly the same. Like me.

AFTER THE MEN
ARE DEAD

WHAT WILL IT BE LIKE WHEN THE MEN IN OUR lives have died? It won't happen for a while, probably. People live longer now. There's even a chance it might not happen at all—to you or to me, anyway. We could go first in a thousand ways: hit by a truck, done in by breast cancer, murdered. But usually, statistically, women outlive men. When a man is a widower, you notice it; you feel there's a story there, a tragedy. "Widower I hate to see. Looks so forlorn," thinks lonely Leopold Bloom watching the pretty girls wading at Sandymount shore. "Some good matronly woman in a porkpie hat to mother him." Chances are, that porkpie hat will track that widower down. An older heterosexual man without a woman is so rare as to be practically inexplicable. He's like the heir to an oil fortune sorting mail at the post office, a Renaissance prince who's wandered into a painting by Edward Hopper: Why is this Lorenzo, this bejeweled magnifico of boundless sexual opportunity, living in this dreary furnished room? What could the matter be, with so many delightful single friends of ours to choose from? But women moving into their sixties, seventies, eighties alone—there's no story there.

When you're young and alone, you spend hours wondering why. Is it you, is it them, you *and* them? I was so lonely in my early twenties I confided in my old professor Bernard Malamud, of all people. Well, he knew a lot of young writers—just possibly some wonderful brilliant boy had recently been telling him how hard it was to meet girls. "Do you think you are able to give yourself to a man?" he asked me. *Give yourself?* But it's not just the old folk who ask questions like that, or think them. Your friends wonder too—you're a topic of endless fascination, an excuse for everyone to display their psychological shrewdness and inside knowledge of your life (your mother used to do *this*, your father never did *that*, remember when you said *something you yourself have totally forgotten?*). Gossip at this level is so subtle and discursive it's almost a kind of literary criticism; it's as if you were the heroine of a great nineteenth-century novel, with layer upon layer of complexity that can be peeled away, revealing a final mystery, an irreducible opacity, like a pearl—although come to think of it, most of those heroines were married. But by deep middle age it isn't you anymore, if it ever was. It's just boring old demography now: it's them.

"Men may run faster," says Mark, my doctor friend, "but

women win the only race that counts." I believe he made
this remark while watching me eat something bad for him.
I already know three women around my age whose husbands were carried off in the great wave of fatal heart
attacks that sweeps across the tennis courts where men of
fifty play. They're furious, these sudden-death widows: How
could he just *stop* like that? Women can die this way too, I
know. Think of Laurie Colwin dying in her sleep at only
forty-eight, wonderful writer, fabulous talker, prickly friend,
so keen on life's everyday pleasures and excitements—cooking, being a mother, analyzing the wedding announcements
in the *Times*—and on doing everything in exactly the right
way, of which there is always only one (*Shake the beef cubes
in a paper bag with flour, salt, and pepper,* I hear her say every
time I make stew, *and buy some fresh herbs, for heaven's sake,
those bay leaves look like they came from the mummy's
tomb*). But mostly it is men who drop dead without warning,
as it is mostly men who die in motorcycle accidents and
fights and dangerous stunts of all kinds, like drug dealing
and fraternity hazing and going to war and being a suicide
bomber. Women just have more sense, and they are made of
more enduring materials, too. More than half the male
members of the Donner party died of cold and starvation,
but three quarters of the females survived, saved by that
extra layer of fat we spend our lives trying to get rid of. Even
in the Middle Ages, when childbirth killed so many, the
older people were mostly women. This posed a theological
quandary: Why did women, clearly the lower sex and the
cause of the Fall to boot, outlive men, their clear superiors,

favored by God? Aristotle had stated very clearly that women died earlier. Could the great authority be wrong? After much debate, scholastics agreed that the answer must have something to do with the Virgin Mary. She had made God like women better, and she had come after Aristotle, hadn't she?

So what will it be like? What will I think about? I can't remember a time since puberty when I wasn't preoccupied with love—looking for it, falling in and out of it, wondering why it made me unhappy, looking for it some more. In my twenties I would read about women who went off on dangerous, dramatic adventures, crossing deserts on camels or sailing across the Atlantic in tiny boats, and I would wonder where they got the self-assurance to cancel so much time from the calendar of romantic possibility. Did those intrepid women know something I didn't about where the great single men had all vanished to? Perhaps they were not to be found at the Poetry Center of the 92nd Street Y after all— they were eating peanut butter from a spoon in midocean or dropping by the oasis for a chat with the local herdsmen. In France I met a woman in her thirties, an artist, who had moved to an abandoned sixteenth-century village in the Pyrenees and was living there alone, restoring a pair of tiny tumbledown stone houses, backpacking her groceries up the mountain like the astonishingly old gnarled peasants who trotted up and down the rocky foot paths like forest elves. She seemed incredibly happy with her painting, her building project, her beautiful blue vistas. Of all her privations— no electricity, no newspaper, no phone, just a smoky fireplace for heat, her only friends the German couple who ran a group of cottages as a primitive bed-and-breakfast—the one that struck me as unimaginable was manlessness. Well, actually not manlessness itself, which was my own usual condition and was not so bad considered day to day, but the possibility of aloneness stretching out into the future like the Pyrenees: as long as she stayed on that mountaintop she had essentially removed herself from the possibility of meeting her soul mate. It didn't occur to me that perhaps she had already met him and that's why she was living among the rocks without so much as a mailbox. Maybe her soul mate was what she wanted to escape.

When I think about how much of my life has revolved around men I can hardly imagine the great silence, like a snowbank, that is to come. The real silence of the individual vanished last loved man, the one whose obituary will perhaps mention me as his "companion," that silly word that makes one sound like a golden retriever or a squire. Even harder to imagine the other silence, the silence of the door closed forever on a whole range of experience. No more wondering what to wear, what to say, how to charm and let oneself be charmed, no more bringing out one's stories, the ones that say, This is what I'm like (what I want you to think I'm like), this is what matters to me (some of it, anyway), and if you don't see why the joke about Moshe the Jewish mountain climber is hilarious, I'm sorry, I won't be able to sleep with you later after all. No more hours on the phone talking about him with women friends and laughing because you sound like such a teenager. No more staying up late listening to each other's old records, no more reading *Don Quixote* to each other in bed, no more sex—strange to think that there will be an actual, specific last time for that. How often do people recognize that moment for what it is, do you think? How often do they say, Well, that's that?

~

Perhaps, as when we were young, we'll use our imaginations. For years I fantasized about marrying a big jolly man of action, someone outgoing and warm and adventurous and fun, full of stories and gladness. I had originally constructed him in adolescence by combining assorted big talkers from the plays of Shaw with a sandy-bearded, pink-faced crinkly-eyed man I had glimpsed in my childhood holding forth at the bar of a nautical-themed restaurant— one of those places where the place mats are laminated sailing charts and the walls are decorated with fishnets and lobster buoys—on a dark rainy afternoon in outer Queens. As the years went by, I dressed the Shavian sea captain up in various high-minded incarnations: I made him a roly-poly bearded doctor working for the poor, a human rights campaigner, a death-penalty lawyer. He was uncomplicated, straightforward, melancholy sometimes because of the nature of his work, which exposed him to so much violence and sorrow, but resilient and basically cheerful and protective, like a husband in a Laurie Colwin novel or a bear in a folktale. I never actually went out with a man like him, the imaginary good father—in real life it was all tormented writers and intellectuals. In fact, I never even met a man like him. The bits and pieces of him I glimpsed in the ones I did meet were just tricks of the light, like thinking someone had a sunny temperament when he was just unobservant, or thinking someone was brave when he was just tall. I haven't thought about that man in years; he must be pretty old by now. Maybe he's dead.

And what about the struggle, will one miss that too? Think how much time women spend trying to turn their men into what they want! More like women—sympathetic listeners, eager tasters of new foods. And more like men— bold takers of charge, not such big babies. It is amazing to think that a man and a woman can ever live together, and even more amazing to think of all the semi-suppressed turmoil behind that common life—the arguments abandoned in the middle because, really, what is the point? The tart reminders; the rolled eyeballs and the sotto voce *hmmmf*; the absolute necessity of employing the words marital counselors tell you must be avoided at all costs, words like "you never" and "you always" and "How's this for an 'I statement': I hate you!" Most of the women I know have spent solid years in a state of low-level exasperation with men, their own and men in general. How infuriating of men to just pick themselves up and slam the door like that, after all this time, while we are still trying to fix them.

And what about the old loves, those other men in one's head? It's not that you've seen them in decades, or think about them much, or even remember exactly what it was about them that made your skin go cold and prickly when you walked past their building or how they were able to make the phone ring in a special, insistent way, as thrilling as a finger pressed on an intimate place. Some people just get to you, even though everything your friends say about them is true. And in a small, etiolated, late-night-on-the-Internet way, those men still do. You look them up and, amazingly, they still exist; their lives have branched and thickened and twisted, just like yours. This one is a beloved doctor to the homeless in a city you've never heard of. He does free tattoo removal at his clinic on Thursdays and publishes articles about the dangers of dumpster diving. That one is an economist and a father of many children with unusual names. The photos on the university Web site look like an actor's head shots: he's still thin, intense, boyish, beautiful, with that same sidelong smile. He's like some academic Dorian Gray: the aging is all in his cramped, tedious papers; they're posted on the Internet too, but you can't get through a single one. A third edits books you have actually read—books littered with typographical errors, if you remember correctly. You could call these men up or e-mail them (*Hi, I was just looking up some data on income-replacement programs in the 1970s, and I came across your name*) but you don't. You have received such e-mails yourself and found them obscurely troubling, as if once again you are failing to come up with the appropriate emotion: you should care about this person who cares for you, but you don't. You wonder if when the old loves die you'll know somehow—as if a gossamer-thin, invisible connecting thread had suddenly sagged, even though that thread was really something only you were holding all along.

Will it be so bad, to live in a world in which the men are gone? Well, not literally gone. There will still be men, of course, but, unless you are a movie star, they'll be too much younger to be interested in you or vice versa. If you do feel a crush on someone younger—your neighbor, your Italian teacher, the new tech guy at the office—you'll be ashamed; it's so pointless you might as well pine for a homosexual. It will be like when I was forty-two and had a crush on a twenty-eight-year-old BBC reporter. I thought I was so obvious—all those tipsy afternoons at the Spain, one of the few truly low dives left in the Village—but when I invited him over it barely registered. How we laughed, my friends and I. *He just doesn't get it, does he?* But actually, he probably did.

In fact, face it, even the men our own age, the ones who survive, will mostly be looking for younger women. Look at the personals: Decrepit Retiree, no teeth, seeks Slim and Sexy 35. You can't even blame them, these old roués; they're only taking advantage of their advantage. You might as well blame a person with good health insurance for seeing their doctor instead of sitting around all day in the emergency room surrounded by cranky babies and gunshot victims. It is like that scene at the end of *On the Beach*, when Peter and Mary, the nice, normal couple, get ready to commit suicide together before radiation sickness finishes them off, and suddenly Peter goes into remission, and even though he knows it's only temporary, a day or two, he's ravenously hungry and full of energy, and it is very hard for him to give that up, to poison the dog and lie down next to his pale, sick wife.

Even when everybody in the world is dead, you might still want to live. So you can understand why a man might want to be with a woman half his age—to touch that velvety skin and look into those clear bright eyes, in which there is none of the knowingness and skepticism of women his own age. Perhaps it's just male propaganda that tells women they don't want the same thing, that women don't care about smooth skin and trim bodies and truly perpendicular erections. Maybe, as in so many areas of life, women have simply learned not to want what they can't have. "You have to train yourself not to see them as your grandfather," said Linda, divorced at fifty-three, of the men who responded to her personals ad. Linda wants me to write about what bastards men are to reject their coevals: "It's not true that they get really young women—they end up with someone nine or ten years younger. Just enough to humiliate women their own age." I'm not so sure—I've been to academic parties where every other couple was a male full professor and a female grad student. But isn't the sensible, dignified position here to simply shower scorn on the old fools and say, Good, let her change his diapers in a few years? I can't imagine being with a much younger man, someone who said "awesome" a lot and remembered what he was doing when he found out that Kurt Cobain was dead. Once on the train I overheard one businessman say to another, "It's like Stalin said, Give them an inch . . ." How could I love someone who didn't see why that was funny, how the whole twentieth century is in that remark—the domestication of European horror by American ignorance, history as whimsical misremembering, as typo? But perhaps my pre-emptive rejection of the young is just defensive snobbism on my part, and the truth is that I can't imagine a younger man accepting my dilapidated body the way, mysteriously, young women lay their glowing selves down next to some wrinkled, dry old tortoise.

Will it be restful, not having to think about love, romance, sex, pleasing, listening, encouraging, smiling at the old jokes—all the small ways and the not-so-small ways women bend themselves to men's expectations, needs, habits, antennae always raised as if for sounds from the baby's room? Men take a lot of attending to and on; there's a lot of putting down of books involved, a lot of turning down of radio just when a story comes on you really want to hear, to say nothing of the day turning into one meal after another. A can of soup is never enough somehow; before you know it you're ordering huge quantities of Chinese food. It would be nice to think that when one has gotten used to it, it will feel like a well-deserved retirement. "Barbara has a woman friend she goes on trips with," I heard one white-haired woman tell another at a classical music concert at our local church. "And this friend said, 'Barbara, between us we've had five husbands and they're all gone.'" And the two old ladies, trim in their good suits and pearls, shrugged their shoulders and laughed.

People are always telling women they can't live without a man—but maybe they say this so often because something so visibly untrue needs to be constantly reinforced, like religion. Oddly, they don't say a man can't live without a woman, although husbands live longer than bachelors. It's obvious that single women manage better than single men, at least the straight men: just compare linen closets, refrigerators, mailboxes; look around yourself at the theater or the museum or any movie starring human beings rather than cars or guns or breast implants. Where are the men while the women are off being civilized? Chasing women. "He's lying," said one friend when I told her the man I lived with had left to be by himself. "Men can't be alone for five minutes." She was right, too. Is it some radical insufficiency, some missing emotional vitamin in men that makes them experience as a personal rejection two women having a glass of wine in a bar after work or a woman reading on a park bench, peacefully twirling her hair and looking forward to the egg salad sandwich in the paper bag beside her? *Why don't they pay attention to me? Bitches*. When I was twenty a man trailed me for blocks in Paris, and when I shook my head no at his offer of a stick of butter to sleep with him he narrowed his eyes with real hatred and muttered *Salope!* Slut.

My husband was furious when a writer friend invited me to an all-female party—for the purposes of the ensuing quarrel, it wasn't supposed to count that he regularly played basketball with a group of men, or that all his colleagues at work were men, attended by women given exciting showbiz titles ("booker," "production manager") so their parents wouldn't think they had spent $200,000 on tuition at Sarah Lawrence so that their daughters could get jobs as secretaries and personal assistants. I thought the single-sex party idea was silly and artificial. I mocked its premise, as if at coed parties we women didn't talk to each other—of course I talked to women! Some of my best friends were women! Yet in the end, I skipped the party to keep peace at home and because actually, come to think of it, talking to men *was* the exciting thing about going to a party. Especially a man you hadn't met yet, who might whisk you away from the man you had, the one you were forgoing the party to please. Perhaps the hostess was right and I was even more man-crazy than she thought.

But that was years ago, when we were drunk on the life force, hunting for fathers for the babies we didn't know we wanted to have. What about now? Women my age, coupled or single, have all-female gatherings all the time—book clubs, movie clubs, political discussion groups, potluck suppers of old college classmates. They mock *Real Simple*, but read it anyway, for its vision of orderly, beautiful domesticity at once practical and elegant, in which the living room is done in muted colors with names like Cloud and Dawn, the children are always sweetly sleeping, and men barely exist. There are no articles in *Real Simple* about how to please a man in bed or the kitchen, how to interpret his silences, how to get him to do what you want, like remember to buy kitty litter or agree to see a therapist or go down on you more often. There is just you, floating through your elegant pre-war apartment or spacious center-hall colonial, arranging a flower here, plumping up a pillow there, before retiring into a bathtub surrounded by lit candles, like a kind of watery altar on which you offer yourself to yourself.

Will we be like the Amazons, after the men are dead? To the Greeks, who dreamed them up, the Amazons were everything decent women were supposedly not, warlike and stoic and high-spirited like men—and isn't it interesting that a group of women without men are thought to be so masculine, when you'd assume they would be most concentratedly feminine? No one pictures a group of men without women—soldiers or sailors or prisoners or pirates—as feminized, even if they have sex with each other. That shows you that femininity is relative; it's about men, in a way that masculinity is not about women. The Amazons cut off their right breasts the better to shoot their arrows; the left they kept for breast-feeding the female infants they conceived in trysts with men from a neighboring tribe, who kept the boys. Meaning: to live without men is a kind of mutilation of femaleness. Yet in myths men are obsessed with these powerful, gallant, self-sufficient women, who possess the very qualities they admire in themselves. Achilles fell in love with Penthesilea and raped her corpse after he killed her in battle; Theseus was mad for Antiope, until he dumped her for Phaedra and killed her when she stormed the wedding. Most of the Amazons whose beautiful, difficult names have come down to us—Aello, Prothoe, Tecmessa—are remembered for being killed by some hero or other.

It would be different if we were twenty or thirty, driving men wild with our estrogen-laced aloofness, but I don't suppose we will be much like the Amazons now, actually, except possibly in monobreastedness. Getting together to read *The*

House of Mirth over five different kinds of pasta salad is not much like hurtling into battle and running your enemies through with a spear. Besides, the men who would be threatened will be dead, or off having sex with their new young mates, in which case they will be relieved that we have found some harmless way of occupying our time, unlike Antiope.

It is so hard to imagine oneself as old, even when one is practically old already. A set of images comes up unbidden: I'm drinking tea from a flowered cup, pottering in the garden in a floppy straw hat, reading Trollope on the porch, talking to my cats, listening to Samuel Ramey, who will probably be dead by then, sing the thrilling last scene of *Don Giovanni.* It's as if age makes one a dotty English spinster, the way my former husband used to wonder when he was a child if a Yiddish accent was something that happened to your voice when you got old. "Fuck the garden," says Anna, my oldest friend. "Let's go to Afghanistan—they respect old people in Asia. I'll start a clinic and you can manage it." No, I say, I can't even manage my cell phone; I'll start a school and teach English. Or is that culturally imperialist? Drinking our skim-milk coffees by the Central Park boathouse, we spin out our fantasy plan. I can almost picture us, wizened and lean in those mirrored dresses they wear, our wispy hair and wrinkled throats swathed in colorful scarves—culturally respectful, but also rather dashing. I picture myself under a canopy, teaching my students to recite from memory the moralizing verses of my childhood. "Into my heart's treasury / I slipped a coin," they chant in unison.

"That time cannot take / Nor a thief purloin. / Oh better than the minting / Of a gold-crowned king / Is the safe-kept memory / Of a lovely thing." And it just might be that the only place on earth where Sara Teasdale is a living poetic presence will be that open-air classroom, and one of those children will be so struck by the word "minting" or the image of the coin tucked safely in its mental hiding place that she will remember that poem all her life, as I have. We'll have to go to a Dari-speaking region, I say, because Pashtun is too difficult to pick up at whatever great age we'll be; in fact, we're probably already several decades past the Pashtun-acquisition stage of life. "Oh, I don't know about that," Anna says. "Edmund Wilson started on Hungarian when he was sixty-five." We begin listing other people who did unusual adventurous things in later life—though, true, most of the famous late starters were younger than we are even now. George Eliot is often cited as coming late to writing, but she was only thirty-nine when she published her first book. There's always Grandma Moses, who began painting at seventy-seven, which would be encouraging except for having people not your grandchildren call you "Grandma." It seems a high price to pay.

It would be a little dangerous; we might even die of some easily curable disease like pneumonia, and think how foolish we would feel then. Or not—I get a vague image of a low bed by a window through which streams dusty deep-golden light. Pneumonia's fairly quick and painless, or at least less painful than the alternatives it saves you from, which is why they used to call it the old man's friend. We'd skip the whole dragged-out hospital death with the tubes and equipment and "procedures" and nurses getting all puritanical with the painkillers, our children feeling guilty if they skipped a day of visiting, always wondering if they pulled the plug too soon or too late, and having to live forever with mental images of their mothers wild-eyed, with fragile sunken faces, like terrified half-starved birds. Wouldn't it be better for them to imagine us as just *away*, so busy and happy and stunned with the beauty and strangeness of our new home we forgot to send them a postcard?

"There they are, telling each other all our secrets," says Anna's husband, Jim, who has walked across the park with Steven to meet us and go on together to the Metropolitan Museum. The men look relaxed and jaunty and remarkably healthy, as if they've just come in from a country walk and are ready for a piece of cake. It's a beautiful October day— the sun shining in an intense blue sky, the air as clear as a pane of glass. Nobody is dying; no one even has a cough. I look at Steven and my heart turns over—I am so moved by his thick glasses, his high vulnerable forehead, with its corona of white flyaway hair. He looks wise and cheerful and immensely clever, like an inventor in a children's book. I have promised to marry him in the spring, in a wedding with lots of flowers.

"Hello, my love," he says, "what are you two conspiring about?"

"Oh, nothing," I say.

MEMOIR OF A SHY PORNOGRAPHER

A LONG TIME AGO, WHEN I HAD JUST FINISHED COL-
lege, I worked as a freelance copy editor and proof-
reader of pornographic novels. My friend Pat, two years out
of Newton College of the Sacred Heart and as lovely as a
Pre-Raphaelite seraph, had gotten me into it. She had found
her way to porn proofing through her job as managing editor of *Gallery*, a soft-core men's magazine, where she made
up the letters for the readers' sex forum because the real letters were too pathetic, illiterate, or weird to print. It seemed
like easy money at the time. Pat would get out her blue
pencil when her train left Penn Station on Friday evening;
by the time she got off in Hudson for a weekend of gar-
dening and cooking with her lawyer boyfriend, she would
be done.

People who say there's no such thing as easy money have a point. You don't know the meaning of tedium until you are midway through correcting the spelling and punctuation in a thirty-page description of fellatio written at breakneck speed by an engineering student trying to make enough money to go to Cancún for spring break. *Thirstily, she wrapped her hungry, vampire-red lips like a Baker SPD open side-pipe vise around his throbbing machinelike...* hmm, take out that second comma, of course, but are vampires red? And can a vise be said to wrap? Doesn't it more, let's see, clamp? Tidying porn prose induced in me a peculiar irritability, almost a kind of claustrophobia—there was the frustration of having to inch word by word along such idiotic sentences, and also the other kind of frustration, which those sentences, despite their idiocy, induced. Still, if I put working on porn together with my other part-time jobs—writing thumbnail reviews of midlist novels for *Publishers Weekly,* reading the newspaper to a blind writer rumored to believe he could tell by smell if a woman was having her period—it made me feel I was having the sort of raffish experience people came to New York to have.

Beeline Books, the publisher for whom Pat and I worked, occupied a featureless suite of offices in a nondescript building on the East Side, over by Bloomingdale's. Blank walls, cheap, nondescript furniture—a block of scratched black file cabinets, a couple of metal desks—gave the place a temporary air, like one of those shady apartment-finder services that would extract a huge fee before sending you out to look at places that had always been rented by the time you got there. There were none of the decorative touches typical of publishing houses—no houseplants or vases of flowers, no framed book jackets, no photos of authors looking soulful with their chins propped on one hand. *(That's Rick Feibleman, you know, Lance Manley? Who writes the Horny Highways series? Great guy!)* There weren't even any books. The staff could have packed up and emptied the entire place in forty-five minutes, which, come to think of it, given the obscenity laws in force at the time, must have been a constant possibility. In fact, perhaps they had decamped before I arrived on the scene, because another thing curiously missing from the offices of Beeline Books was people. The only person I ever saw when I went in to pick up or bring back my assignments was Cheryl, the managing editor. Cheryl was tall and good-humored and spoke with a Texas drawl. She dressed in crisp white man-tailored shirts, wore her straight brown hair in a no-fuss ponytail, and gave off a mixture of incongruous social signals, like a cheerleader moonlighting as a secretary, or possibly a secretary who had become an editor by default, when the real editors had gone into hiding. She paid seventy-five dollars for copyediting a manuscript and thirty-five for proofreading galleys, and it was steady, mindless work. I would take my bundle of paper back to my tiny apartment on Riverside Drive, which had a wisp of a view of the river if I pushed the old brown chair in the bedroom up against the window at just the right angle and was high enough up so that the bottles my neighbors liked to toss out the window into the courtyard sounded like coins hitting bottom in a deep, deep well. With a pot of strong coffee and a Cadbury fruit-and-nut milk-chocolate bar I could march my eyes down those arid, choked, and tangled sentences for just about an hour at a time before I had to stop or scream. *Jack snaked his hand toward Tawny's invitingly swelling nipple, it's pink aureole glistening with delicate feminine sweat, her tongue darting among her teeth like a string of pearls.* Okay, make that "its," "areola," "between" instead of "among," but, uh-oh, shouldn't that be *two* strings of pearls, one for upper teeth and one for lower? And wasn't Tawny called Linda a few pages ago? A young and dashing William Butler Yeats looked up at me reproachfully from the cover of the paperback *Selected Poems and Two Plays* open on the floor, as if to say, *What's happened to you? I thought we had an understanding.*

On the plus side, unlike the writers I had encountered in a brief stint proofreading at *Esquire*—short men who swaggered through the office like Latin American generals and whose names I still remember by the linguistic atrocities that used to send us, the women of the copy desk, into fits of resentful hilarity—the authors at Beeline never complained if you fixed up their prose a bit as you went along. They never said things like "I used 'thrusting' ten times in two pages on *purpose,* it's part of my *rhythm.*" And Cheryl never complained if you missed a typo or let the writer spell it "come" and "cum" on the same page, which surely I must have done many times. Interestingly, in order to stretch a description of a single sex act out to the length Beeline required—twenty or thirty pages, which took as long to read as the actual real-life activities would or sometimes, in my limited experience, quite a bit longer——the Beeline writers had hit upon the very techniques pioneered by the giants of high modernism: stream of consciousness, internal monologue, indirect discourse, dream sequences, disruptions of time, and far too many adjectives. Sometimes, when I saw a single sentence throbbing and thrusting down a whole page and maybe the next one too, I would cheat a bit and just kind of sweep over it with my eyes. I did the same thing with *The Sound and the Fury* and *The Waves.*

~

Now, of course, what seems striking and makes this story seem like it took place in a garret in the nineteenth century is that there was a time when pornography was something you read. Beeline books were made of words——there weren't even any illustrations. They were literature, produced like other books: conceived, written, edited, proofread, printed. The uniform covers of tasteful olive green for the incest series would have done for a paperback edition of the Brontës. I didn't have a clear idea of who actually read Beeline books——teenage boys? Lonely sailors? But whoever that reader was, he mentally re-created the scene on the page——let's say Dr. Sexalot's double seduction by the pair of bewitching nurses he finds canoodling in the emergency room supply closet——through the same process of imagination Lionel Trilling would use to conjure up Helen and Margaret Schlegel at the symphony, or Natasha eloping with Anatol in the snow. In fact, the porn reader had to work a lot harder than Trilling, because the very mental processes required to bring one of those garbled scenes to life (*hugely, he stoked his cylindrical redness into her teeming honeypot*) would, if he was successful, naturally make him want to throw the book down and act it out right then and there. Surely few Beeline customers waded all the way through a thirty-page sex passage before tearing off their clothes and ravishing themselves. The point of reading pornography was to be unable to keep reading: "unput-downable" was not a compliment. Some French literary theorist could make a whole career out of that paradox. Beeline probably could have published the same manuscript over and over with minor adjustments and nobody would have noticed. Or would they have received complaints? *Dear Sirs, I demand a refund for the enclosed copy of* More Sex for Sandra, *which, barring a few trivial details, is the exact same book as the far superior (to my mind)* Mandy's Climax! *You can imagine my outrage at discovering this in midocean....* Unlike watching a porn video, reading porn involved a lot of fantasy—your Brandy, *bosoms plunging as a volcanic organism swept through her like a tidal wave,* wouldn't be, couldn't be exactly like mine. Thus, although reading took more work than watching—for example, you had to know how to read and have a vocabulary well over five hundred words, not counting four-letter ones—it offered more freedom and power. As reading-response theorists would soon argue, reading is always a two-way street, always an act of the imagination. Books didn't raise the disturbing labor issues posed by videos, either. You didn't have to wonder if Misty and Candy were sex slaves or if Brianna did that scene with

the dog because some slimeball producer promised to introduce her to Martin Scorsese.

~

At the time what struck me as strange and interesting and
novel about this job, and what I loved to make into funny
stories for my friends, was the sort of setting in which
Beeline books took place. For all the confused anarchy of the
prose, in which there sometimes seemed to be more organs
and orifices than characters to attach them to, the books followed a set of formal written guidelines as strict and in their
way as wholesome as the ones for Harlequin romances. No
little children, no rape, no sadomasochism, no necrophilia—
or, come to think of it, any other predilections ending in
philia—and no racial slurs; plus, there had to be characters,
a location, and a plot. The very existence of these rules suggested a wider, darker sea of porn, of which I was paddling
in the safest of shallows, but I was too naïve to see that then.
I thought all porn took place in the world of Beeline:
Whitepeoplelandia, with its hearty, clean-cut men and
bland, compliant women, where everyone was Christian and
suburban and drank moderately of beer and the only meal
anyone ate was steak and salad. Even the incest plots had a
gee-whiz provincial quality, something like: Brad White, a
middle manager with Baker Vise, takes his trim, perky-
breasted wife, Tammy, on a trip to New York with their
teenagers, Bob and Jess, and who should they run into having steak and salad in Times Square but Tammy's volup-
tuous sister and muscular brother-in-law, Pam and Chad,

and the twins, Tiffany and Jan! Zany couplings and triplings ensue, as how could they not? You could write it yourself in a weekend, if you wanted a Mexican vacation badly enough. Sometimes Pat and I talked about writing a novel ourselves, but we never got much further than the title: *Going Down on the Farm*, the story of two gorgeous and frustrated city girls who flee their lackluster boyfriends to house-sit in the country, where they end up having wild sex with dozens of unbelievably attractive and attentive local he-men. Our pen name was to be Dawn Redwood, which was a kind of private joke because Dawn was a typical submissive-sounding porn girl's name, but "dawn redwood" is the name of a beautiful tree.

~

Why did I do it? Today one would hardly ask the question. Pornography is everywhere——in your in-box, on the newsstand, on the pay-per-view channel in your hotel room. Jenna Jameson, porn star and best-selling author, is respectfully profiled in the *New York Times*. Watching sex videos or making your own is mainstream middle-class behavior, the next step after pink lightbulbs and crotchless panties and the other helpful hints in those ubiquitous articles about how to put the sizzle back in your marriage. It's the people who have a problem with porn——even a simple aesthetic revulsion at the shaved and implanted phoniness of it all—— who are suspect now, and who have to prove their normality by insisting that they "like sex," as if sex were all one thing, like oatmeal. Imagine if you said, Yes, I like sex, with the right person, in the right place, in the right mood, preferably after a lovely meal cooked by someone else; otherwise, frankly, I'd rather get on with *Daniel Deronda*. You'd sound like a fetishist, someone who needs outlandish props and sets to feel excited—food! wit! clean sheets! affection!—because excited is the way porn tells us people feel all the time. In porn, no one takes a night off, no one even rejects one partner for another they like better; they just have them both at once, and the meter reader, too, should he happen to drop by. When porn came in books, its vision of sex was clearly a fantasy, something some odd duck of a writer dreamed up out of his head. Now that it's filmed, it looks more like a documentary: actual live human beings are enacting those extravagant scenes. You can forget that what you are seeing is still a scripted fantasy, designed around the requirements of its medium and the vanities of its consumers as surely as a Beeline plot. People in porn films do things because they show up well on-screen, not because people actually do them in real life, at least not until they've watched a lot of porn.

Back then, though, pornography was still basically smut—secret, silly, a little bit shameful. The official line was that it was for losers—men who couldn't get real women—unlike today, when it's for men who don't want real women. The opposition to it was religious and small-town; to sophisticated urban liberals, porn was basically trivial and fun. In the 1960s my parents subscribed to *Eros*, Ralph Ginzburg's arty soft-core magazine, which was shut down, so my father always said, after it featured an interracial couple. Behind the other books in my mother's bedside cabinet I discovered *Fanny Hill,* which offered a far more compelling picture of eighteenth-century England than did the Sir Roger de Coverley Papers, which we were struggling through in Mrs. Elliston's tenth-grade English class, and *The Perfumed Garden of Sheikh Nefzaoui,* which discoursed endlessly on what women wanted in a man's "crupper" and "verge," and offered such advice as "Do not drink rain-water directly after copulation, because this beverage weak-ens the kidneys." Owning such books was a lighthearted thing, a way of showing how far one had come from West Virginia or Borough Park. You didn't have to have a political position about it. That came later, when feminists accused pornography of promoting degrading views of women and encouraging sexual violence.

Pat's brother arranged for us to see *Deep Throat* in his office after work, and it didn't occur to us to wonder if some-one off-screen was waving a gun at Linda Lovelace, as she later said had been the case. After all, she had visited *Esquire,* looking pretty and giddy and pleased with herself in a long green hippie-princess dress; the men in the office had never looked so dull and desperate. But we didn't see her as a role model of liberation, either. We just assumed she was some sort of odd exhibitionist, another New York char-acter. Now we sat transfixed, alternately wide-eyed with shock and bursting with laughter. A woman whose clitoris is in her throat, so she has orgasms—multiple orgasms—from oral sex! As a rationale for male selfishness, *Deep Throat* was pure Beeline. After all, the deepest fantasy level at Beeline—

deeper than the one about every woman wanting wild sex all the time, and the one about boring ordinary life as the thinnest veneer hiding a perpetual orgy, and the one about fantastically beautiful women aflame with desire for the Brads and Chads of Whitepeoplelandia—was the idea, the wish, the delusion that a man can satisfy a woman simply by satisfying himself. That is what marked porn as being not explicit writing about sex but representations of male sex fantasies, masturbatory aids for unimaginative men. A man could read porn his whole life and never learn a thing about real women: how to talk to them, what they liked, where, if the clitoris was not actually located in their throat, the damn thing was.

But a woman could read those books and learn a thing or two about men, and that, I think, is the true explanation of why I worked for Beeline. Bizarre as it seems, since of course I knew I was reading male fantasies—the fantasies, more-over of some verbally inept Rick or Ron, half-empty white cartons of Chinese food heaped at his feet as he forged ahead through the night on his marathon of typing—I was look-ing for information. Not facts; I'd read *Everything You Always Wanted to Know About Sex*, so I felt I had enough of those, and anyway facts about sex—secretions, engorge-ments—sounded so unappealing, so medical. What I wanted was something more individual, more interior, more transforming, but also raw, direct, and male, not prettified and blurry "erotica" like Anaïs Nin's. I had heard Nin speak my senior year in college, a still-willowy old woman in chalk-white pancake makeup, wearing a long puffy-sleeved dress made out of an Indian bedspread. When she warned us not to let feminism take away our womanly mystery, she lost me forever; she sounded like some Victorian church lady arguing against giving women the vote. Why did so many people want women to be mysterious? Nobody advised men to wrap themselves up in images and secrets. And yet men did. Even Henry Miller, whose stock-in-trade was sexual truth telling and whose collected works I devoured after reading Kate Millett's denunciation of him in *Sexual Politics,* was too stuck on his own myth to be quite believable. Could that scene with the carrot really have happened? Maybe he should have taken a pseudonym, like Lance Manley.

I wanted information about men. What were they really like? What did they want? How did sex look and feel to them? It wasn't that I thought I was getting the literal, physical truth from Rick and Ron, exactly. I hadn't had a lot of experience—in fact, I had had practically none that mattered, none that seemed more than parts from Baker Vise fitting together more or less awkwardly and embarrassingly—but I had had enough to know that a woman didn't really feel *thunderous torrents of molten sperm splashing against her quivering cervix.* That was just a literary convention, like seventeenth-century love poems to girls with names like Chloe and Belinda. But one of the things that came through that hopeless thicket of ill-chosen words that was Beeline was desire: men wanted women's bodies, and they wanted those bodies the way they actually were—smells, wetness, pubic hair. The adjectives of praise the authors heaped on these and other feminine parts were hackneyed, and most of them would have done equally well for food: *hungrily, he breathed in the spicy, cinnamon scent that wafted from the thick brown pelt surmounting her delicate labias*—hmm . . . surmounting? labias? But underneath the hapless language and haphazard punctuation were neediness and gratitude, as if it was enough for a woman, any woman, just to be willing to take off her clothes and get into bed. It seems so quaint now, when, so I'm told, every man under forty expects a woman to wax away her pubic hair. It's like Afros and the Adelle Davis cookbook, like a lonely sailor in his cabin, reading by the light of a swinging lamp.

~

There was something else I wanted too: a way out of my shyness and inexperience and embarrassment and fear and prudishness and standoffishness and excessive romanticism—all of which coexisted with my interest in sex, which was as consuming as that felt by all those fictional Brads and Chads, but which I was unable to express in my lived life. I simply could not bring together the real world and the world that was in my head: the world in which I avoided answering the phone for days because I didn't know how to turn a man down for a date without hurting his feelings, and the world in which I rode the Broadway local and played the game of choosing which of the men in the car— or even which *two* men—I would have sex with, if, due to some highly improbable, Lance Manleyesque plot twist, I had to choose.

The logical way to shed these inhibitions and resolve these contradictions would have been to sleep with more people, but to do that I would have had to like men who liked me instead of men who liked someone else. For assorted reasons—going to a girls' school, a penchant for unrequited crushes, automatic rejection of men who said "groovy" or used the word "ball" as a verb—I had missed the sixties, and half the seventies too. Why, I would ask myself, would I want to sleep with someone I didn't particularly want to have dinner with? Besides, the men who liked me tended to be even more tied up in knots than I was— I was their idea of a free spirit. Take Carl, who was getting his Ph.D. in English at Columbia and who on what proved to be our final date confided to me that thanks to his therapist he'd realized that his aversion to chicken was a projection of his repressed jealousy of his younger brother, who as a baby had borne a remarkable resemblance to a roaster. I could see what he meant—the plumpness and compactness and yellowy pinkness—but sleep with Carl? It would be like going to bed with Little Hans.

~

And so, ever the devoted student, I read. I read *Maggie Goes South* and *Virgins in Uniform* and *The Temptress on the 23rd Floor* and *Cadillac Orgy* and *Mistress of Mischief* and many more. Some of the scenes were disturbing—a scene with a garage mechanic and a grease gun haunted my imagination for years. And all of it was boring to the point of madness. But what is boring, when it comes to books? I would never have gotten through *Pamela* and *Clarissa* had I not been on jury duty, condemned to sit for two weeks on a bench with nothing else to do, yet those cinder-block-sized monuments to sententiousness were the toast of the nation's English departments. As Lionel Trilling would have been the first to point out, entertainment isn't everything.

The remarkable thing about reading all that pornography was that, in a way, it worked. After months and months of forging through endless ham-fisted descriptions of Brad and Chad performing every conceivable sex act with Tammy and Pam, things that had seemed weird and distasteful and threatening, like oral sex, seemed ordinary, like steak and salad, just what men and women did in Whitepeoplelandia, and probably not only there. Jimmy Walker was wrong when he said that no girl was ever ruined by a book. It had taken a lot more books than one, but I was that girl.

~

A while ago, I saw a Beeline book on one of those blankets homeless people lay down on upper Broadway to display the bits of flotsam they put up for sale. It was tattered and smudged and looked as if it had been retrieved from the garbage. In fact, lying there next to a decrepit copy of *What Color Is Your Parachute?* and a jumble of grubby Happy Meal toys, it looked like it had not quite made it all the way out of the trash. Who buys this stuff, I wondered, other homeless people? Do they have some kind of barter system: I'll trade you this purple scrunchie for that NYU mug with the chipped handle? The book had a publication date long after my time, but I thought of taking it home anyway, for old times' sake. Only when I leafed through it, I felt as depressed as if I had opened a refrigerator full of old bologna sandwiches. There, indeed, were the Whitepeople-landian couplings and triplings I remembered, the familiar tormented logorrheic prose—all neatly punctuated and properly spelled. But the combination of cluelessness and clumsiness that was a Beeline trademark no longer seemed so amusing. The men seemed nasty and calculating, the women passive and dumb. The story, an incest plot, was more sinister than those I remembered, too. The anything-goes uncles had become molesting fathers. Had Beeline gone more hard-core to compete with the new visual media? Or had the uncles always been fathers but I'd skimmed over that as I had over those dense, incomprehensible wodges of sexual description? Perhaps I was more like an ordinary porn reader than I wanted to believe, and out of those grim and unpromising materials had constructed my own fantasy, one of reassurance and approval and safety and pleasure.

I'd kept a finished copy of only one of the books I'd worked on. It was called *Alicia's Love Lessons*, by Rod Strong, and I'd saved it because it was so much better than the others. It involved a male teacher at a girls' boarding school and his seduction by his provocative student Alicia and her many equally eager classmates. The characters were vivid—the hero, who had washed up on the farther shores of Waspitude after a rather knockabout life, had the exact mixture of humorous detachment and well-meaning pas-sivity I had encountered in the few male teachers I'd known in high school—and the writing was clever and sexy and sly. If it weren't for the required twenty-page descriptive passages recurring in all their deadly minutiae after every turn in the story, it would have been a good book. Even the sex scenes were readable—at least, I read them.

Brian, the author of *Alicia's Love Lessons*, was the only Beeline writer I ever met. Cheryl had told me he was a hopeless alcoholic, perhaps even dying, who had gone home to live with his mother as his last chance for survival; one Saturday morning she called to say that he was so far past deadline he was coming right over to deliver his just-finished manuscript directly to me. The man who rang my doorbell an hour later was a skinny wreck with yellow skin and terrible teeth, and he clearly had not lived in Whitepeoplelandia for some time. He stood in my doorway like an avatar of ruin and knowledge, smiling a rueful smile. The combination of sex and death—attraction, embarrassment, pity, and fear, but especially attraction—was just too much for me. To this day I regret not inviting him in.

Maybe Cheryl was right and he died before long. That would explain why Rod Strong wrote no more books for Beeline. Maybe, though, he went on to become the beloved author of cult science-fiction novels who has his same real name. He was probably no more than forty when I met him, so it's just possible that he pulled himself together and turned to spinning out fantasies of a different but hardly more improbable sort. Maybe porn had served his purposes by then, whatever they were, as it was soon to have served mine. It's a common name, though. He could be anywhere.

Alicia's Love Lessons, on the other hand, is definitely somewhere in my apartment, stowed in a safe place so my daughter won't find it—a place so safe I can't remember where it is. I imagine it will turn up someday—at least I hope it will. After all these years, I'd like to read it again.

BEAUTIFUL
SCREAMER

I WAS ECSTATIC WHEN MY DAUGHTER WAS BORN.
Beside myself. I didn't care that I'd had a cesarean,
although I would have liked more Demerol afterward. I
didn't even care that the operation was unnecessary, the
result, as Lissa, my obstetrician, acknowledged, of a lab mistake. "You're strong enough to handle this," she told me
when she dropped by my hospital room a few days later with
the news. "You can take it." Lissa and her partner, Jane,
were beautiful, slender, delicate dark-eyed women—they
looked like they had been antelopes in a previous life. They
wore high heels and little black dresses under their white
coats and stocked their waiting room with *Town & Country*;
you felt they should be drinking martinis at the Beekman
instead of sticking their hands up your vagina. My main

goal at every prenatal visit was to to get Lissa to promise not to give me an episiotomy; to me this represented all the horror and humiliation of childbirth, being slit open like an animal, butterflied like a chicken on the grill. She would politely accept the articles I had cut out for her from *Science News* and *Family Planning Perspectives* and promise that she would never perform one unnecessarily. As it turned out, she kept her word. I had the unnecessary C-section instead.

But so what? Mistakes happen. I had Sophie, that was the important thing. When the nurse put her in my arms, I looked into her eyes and it was like looking into a pair of morning glories. They were that blue, that clear, that open. I felt we understood each other completely, as if Plato was right and we arrive on earth full of knowledge and that this was the very moment, right here in the operating room, before she began to forget. It was as if my mother and grandmothers had sent her to me from that other world. What difference did it make how she'd gotten here? It baffled me how women got into childbirth perfectionism, blaming themselves if they couldn't give birth vaginally, or if in the end, despite the childbirth preparation classes, despite meditations and mantras and visualization and breathing and exercise and monitoring of diet and always remembering to avoid words like "pain" and "unbearable" in favor of words like "discomfort" and "tired," they went for the painkillers. "I had an epidural," one new mother confided in me as we shuffled along the hospital corridor in our bathrobes. She laughed nervously. "I hope my baby will be all right." Having a baby was machismo for women; it was like becoming a Marine. You couldn't be a sissy, a wimp, a girl. Because it wasn't about you: it was about doing what was best for your child. Anything that went wrong in that department was your fault. In this respect pregnancy and childbirth were psychological boot camp for motherhood: anything that went wrong there was going to be your fault too.

I had resisted the competitive-sport aspects of labor and delivery—you are the athlete, your husband is the coach—but I was as susceptible to guilt as any other educated middle-class woman. Never mind that I had researched and written articles debunking the insistence on total abstention from alcohol during pregnancy, as if one drink at mealtime would turn your child into a cabbage. Look at the wine-loving Italians, the Spanish, the French! Years later, when my funny, clever, talkative daughter scored only average on the IQ tests she had to take for kindergarten, my first thought was, It must have been that New Year's Eve champagne before I knew I was pregnant—rather a lot of champagne, if truth be told—that Chianti with pizza at the Marionetta, that beer with the Chinese takeout. Never mind that I had also researched and written articles about the fallacy of IQ. When the psychologist who had done the tests called weeks later to say that he'd made a computational error and Sophie's actual score was "in the gifted range," I felt the way you'd feel when your jury comes back with a verdict of not guilty, after a trial in which the prosecutor was so brilliant you'd started to believe him yourself. Maybe you shot your husband and just forgot. Maybe you embezzled that money in your sleep. "Hey," the psychologist said when I reminded him of the many hundreds of dollars we'd paid for his services, "I didn't have to call you. I'm being nice to you." It was as if he knew I had been willing to kill off my daughter's brain cells. I wasn't innocent. I was just lucky.

~

My friends who were mothers had seemed mildly alarmed when I told them I was pregnant. Perhaps they wondered how I would manage, given that I had never taken care of anything larger than a cat—well, two cats, actually, which isn't as easy as it sounds. It just didn't seem to me that raising a baby was so complicated. People had been doing it for years! True, according to the child-care experts whose books began to pile up by the bed, they hadn't been doing a very good job: there were definite right and wrong ways to feed an infant, play with it, socialize it, keep it warm and clean and happy and curious. But what did the experts know? Didn't the whole field revise itself totally every decade or so? Feed on a schedule—no, feed on demand! The experts were mostly men, anyway, whose wives did the daily work of raising the kids. On the other hand, at least the men took the trouble to be twinkly and avuncular. Penelope Leach, the only famous woman expert, was a dragon, the infant-care equivalent of Margaret Thatcher or Barbara Woodhouse, who had that dog-training show on television ("No bad dogs—only inexperienced owners!"), and you couldn't dismiss her as just another man laying down the law. She was a mother herself; a better mother than you, because she never seemed to have a minute in which raising children was not the foremost thing on her mind. She wrote that you had to talk to your baby when you were pushing the stroller and that not to do so was rude because if the baby was a grown-up you would make conversation. She wrote that if you had a job and the baby was happy you had still done the wrong thing, you had just gotten away with it. Penelope Leach had quite a bit of useful information, which she delivered in a brisk, friendly way, but that was just to cozy you along. Like the men, she obviously thought that if you ignored her advice you'd produce an addict or a killer or a C student—but if that was true the human race would never have survived all those millennia living in mud huts on a diet of lentils and goat milk. Although come to think of it, perhaps inadequate child-rearing practices explained the plethora of addicts and murderers and C students through-out world history. Maybe Hitler's parents had failed to sup-ply him with a black-and-white mobile for his crib. It's not as if human beings were so great.

When Sophie went for her six-month checkup, our pedi-atrician urged me to get a copy of Dr. Richard Ferber's *Solve Your Child's Sleep Problems*. But she doesn't have any sleep problems, I protested. "Well, she will," the doctor said wearily. "Just you wait." Dr. Ferber proposed training your baby to sleep through the night alone by letting her cry without comforting her for longer and longer periods. This was called "Ferberizing," which sounded like some new way of waxing your car. I was quite sure parents would never have Ferberized their babies back in the mud huts. The whole family would all have slept together in a warm smelly heap. I wasn't up to the rigors of Ferberization. It seemed so cold and mean. Sophie could learn to cry herself to sleep when she grew up, like everybody else.

When Sophie woke up and fussed I scooped her up and walked her around the apartment. "Beautiful screamer, wake unto me," I would sing. "Starlight and moonbeams are waiting for thee." Sometimes I would take her into the bed I shared with my husband and we would fall asleep together. According to the experts, this would produce a relaxed and confident baby who trusted her parents to respond to her distress—or a needy, manipulative user who would expect her parents to be at her beck and call for life. What was amazing, too, was that these know-it-alls were not in the least disturbed by their disagreements, even when their opposing advice was placed side by side in magazine features with titles like "We Asked the Experts" and "You Wanted to Know." They just sailed on, blithely asserting their wisdom, like political pundits. The important thing, after all, wasn't to give the right answer. It was to train parents to see child raising as a set of technical problems they couldn't solve on their own, and never to have the thought that perhaps the reason for the conflicting answers was that the questions weren't all that important; whatever you decided was probably all right. The whole child-care-advice industry was about the production and soothing of anxiety, like those women's magazines where the five-day all-tomato weight-loss diet sits right next to the recipe for double-chocolate Oreo pie, and the article listing ten steps to a new you is followed by the one about accepting yourself as you really are.

~

Looking back, I can see that I became depressed. It wasn't baby blues, or, as we now medicalize it, postpartum depression. It was loneliness. In the way that we prepare for ourselves the bed we most don't want to lie in, I had put myself in exactly the position I had spent my life avoiding: I went from being a writer who worked at home to being a stay-at-home wife. My husband was a conscientious father, but he worked long hours and wrote a book on the weekends. My friends, who had had their babies earlier, were back at work. Instead of spending time with people I knew and liked, I had playdates with neighbors. I had always felt guilty about not writing enough; now I felt guilty about hiring a sitter so that I could sit at my desk not writing at all. It didn't really matter, though, that I wasn't getting anything accomplished, because I had nothing to say. Interestingly, no one asked me anymore what I was working on. Once a woman gives birth it's considered impolite, as if you're implying that having a baby isn't enough.

Had anyone inquired that first year, I had my answer ready: *I read the* New York Times *every day. If I die tomorrow, you can put that on my tombstone.* As soon as Cendra took Sophie out for a walk, instead of dashing to my study and getting to work, like the stalwart mother-writers I admired, Margaret Drabble and Harriet Beecher Stowe and

Sylvia Plath—well, okay, bad example—I sank into that
thick gray soup of processed verbiage like an exhausted
insomniac drifting, finally, into drugged slumber. I read the
unsigned editorials about sewage treatment and the
Japanese trade deficit, the obituaries of aged grandparents
named Ida and Sidney (mourned by daughters Linda and
Barbara and grandchildren Arielle, Jeremy, and Zack), the
"Metropolitan Diary," with its familiar returning characters: the wisecracking taxi driver, the gallant doorman, the
cheerful homeless guy. I read the real-estate section to measure our apartment's decline in value and the book review to
measure my own decline in value. I read the fashion pages
to reassure myself that even if I could lose my pregnancy
weight there were no clothes in existence that I could
remotely imagine myself wearing except the clothes I
already had. I read everything but the travel section.
Because what would have been the point of that?

It's not entirely true that I wrote nothing at all. I wrote
dozens, possibly even hundreds of drafts of one poem. It was
called "White Curtains," and I was never able to make
it come right. It started out well enough: *White curtains
wafting and stirring at my bedroom window / in the clear
sunlight at the beginning of spring.* Well, maybe take out
"wafting"; words like "wafting" were definitely part of the
problem. But the poem's real difficulty, of which "wafting"
was only a symptom, was the ungraspable nature of its subject. Something about the way life produces moments of
beauty that seem to be about to reveal a mystery, but never
do? *How much we want such things to mean more than them-*

selves. But they don't mean more? Which is related to the way the death of a loved person has no affect on the on-goingness of the world? *Here is the unmade bed, the half-drunk glass / the book left carelessly open.* Rereading that poem, in its many typed drafts that look so old-fashioned now, like letters from the Second World War, with those thick black serifs and clouded *O*'s and the paper gently puffed around each letter, what strikes me is how effortful it seems, how labored and heavy and dead. It's as if every line was the beginning of a thought I could neither complete nor connect to another thought, it had been dragged up with so much difficulty from some murky but insufficiently deep part of my imagination. Although it was miles away from what really preoccupied me—the baby, my deteriorating marriage, the day-to-day routine in which I felt so swamped— I see that the poem expressed exactly my state of mind, in its leadenness, its fragmented attention, its sadness that seemed to come from outside the careful, elevated language of the poem, like darkness seeping in through the window behind the lamp and the bowl of flowers.

This was my dilemma, as I saw it: motherhood was such an intense experience, it was so important, so necessary, it placed you at the hot center of life, like a coal in fire. At the same time, it marginalized you totally. You became invisible, a function, a means. When I was childless, it was obvious to me that mothers got the shaft. From the kitchen window of our little Greenwich Village apartment I would watch the mothers pushing the toddlers in their strollers to the preschool down the block. The kids were scrubbed and rosy, dressed in adorable outfits—heathery purple and buttery yellow, bubble-gum pink and Granny Smith apple green; in the cold weather they wore thick jackets in bright primary colors and clever knitted hats that made them look like baby Vikings, or jesters, or lion cubs. The mothers trudged behind them in dull baggy sweats, like the Econowives in *The Handmaid's Tale:* they could be their children's servants, or the black-clad stagehands you're not supposed to notice handling those elaborate Indonesian paper puppets.

Once I had a baby of my own, I found out more about why those women looked so grim. It is really hard to go through your regular day with a stroller and baby in tow: shopping in crowded supermarket aisles or tiny cramped Korean greengroceries where everyone looked embarrassed for you if the baby fussed, and hanging the groceries off the back of the stroller, which sometimes tipped over, sending the baby backward looking *very* surprised; muscling up and down the subway stairs and through the turnstiles, which were too narrow, so you had to either lift the stroller over or wait for the token booth clerk to buzz you through the door and whoops, there goes your train. Sometimes people helped, mostly older Hispanic men or fellow mothers, but mostly not, and according to an op-ed in the *New York Times* by one of the new anti-feminist women writers who were coming into vogue, this inconsiderateness was due to legal abortion. Apparently people wanted to help mothers only if they thought the mothers had not chosen their condition. If you had volunteered, you were on your own. This philosophy was in evidence even at the post office, which I noticed for the first time had a sign banning strollers and carriages from the premises. The government, it would seem, did not believe that mothers were entitled to buy stamps or send a package. How I fumed about that! Didn't the stroller ban violate my constitutional right to equal access to government services? Did they think I had no business to transact, or expect my husband to transact it for me? This was Manhattan, not Riyadh. I was like someone suddenly confined to a wheelchair who notices for the first time all the potholes and high curbs.

It wasn't the physical hurdles that bothered me, though—as soon as I escaped the fug and mess of the apartment, I felt full of energy and zest. It took so much preparation to leave the house, I had to put together so many supplies and remember so many things and go back so many times for some forgotten item—diapers! goldfish crackers! Milosh the filthy beloved boy-baby doll!—that by the time I was actually out on the sidewalk I felt as excited and stalwart and determined as a polar explorer. What got to me was the sense of exclusion, of no concessions or accommodation or even acknowledgment. It was as if raising a child was just an odd personal hobby, like unicycling. At the same time, it made you fair game for public comment, even before birth. "It's a boy!" a homeless man assured me on the street. "That's great," another man said, pumping a fist in approval. "You're doing just what you should be doing." Who asked him? "Her feet are cold," a grandmotherly woman remarked as she passed by on the street, the first time we took Sophie out in her stroller. "Where are her shoes?" Other passersby weighed in too: "She needs a hat." "She looks tired." "Poor little girl." And then—this is the awful part—you notice you are doing the same thing with other people's babies. Once I managed to work myself up into a major worry-fit because I saw a baby left in a carriage on the street in front of a brownstone. Obviously, the mother had just dashed inside for a moment, but I stayed and waited till she came back out. I made sure she saw me, too.

~

I kept thinking there must be some way to turn it around and reverse the valences. Instead of making you less powerful, less central, motherhood should make you more so— more connected to others, more part of the swim and swirl. Surely there were societies in which that was true. Hadn't there been some Indian tribe where the mothers made the big decisions? You should radiate heat and power like the sun. You had done, were doing, this great thing! You had profound revelations all the time, like when you realized that if you could sacrifice your life to save your child you would not only do it without hesitation, you would be grateful for the opportunity. Grateful! Imagine feeling that for another person. I could look at Sophie's face for hours; it barely seemed possible that someone so beautiful could exist. Sometimes I felt guilty about the sheer delight I took in her: if I had gotten one of those big-headed lumpy babies that look like Winston Churchill, would I love my child as much? I was so afraid she might have died of crib death during the night that I used to make my husband go into her room before me in the morning. This was the secret emotional life of mothers, and fathers too. "I would drink her pee," my friend Nick said of his baby girl. Shouldn't these deep currents of feeling connect us to each other, adults to children, parent to parent? True, in small ways they do. Suddenly you have something to talk to strangers about, the way men bond over sports—the gloomy guy in the basement at the Strand who prices the used books, Mr. Kim the dry cleaner, the super's bad-tempered wife. The Strand guy's wife was pregnant! Mr. Kim wrote poetry! In the elevator, the super's wife lets a smile flicker across her stern Albanian face. People are nicer to you if you are with a baby. Women on the street always smile at each other's children, and sometimes at each other, too. But it is a rueful, brave-soldier kind of smile, as if to say, Well, we've managed so far.

~

Fortunately, I loved breast-feeding. Sure, for the first month it felt like being bitten by foxes, but after that it was more just a fizzy feeling, like having breasts full of champagne. It wasn't a sexual feeling exactly, but it was definitely sensual, and the closeness and warmth of the baby was sensual too— her soft skin, her heavy head, her hot milky breath, the way she lay back, sated. That breast-feeding is exciting is something you're not supposed to talk about—in fact, a few years after Sophie weaned herself, a woman upstate lost custody of her child for a year when she told a breast-feeding hot-

line that she sometimes felt aroused while nursing—
because God forbid a mother should get a little pleasure for
herself along the way. By then, doctors had even stopped
advising women to drink Guinness to help bring down the
milk, a delightful home remedy that let you feel like Molly
Bloom. Breast-feeding was another thing that had been
turned from a source of power and pleasure into an occasion
for guilt and self-doubt. "I'll never be as close to my child
again," intoned the soft, mournful Kotex-ad-style voice-over
in the La Leche League video we watched in Lamaze class;
never mind that the child in question looked ready to pick
up a backpack and trot off to middle school. Why couldn't
they just say, Some women really enjoy this, why not give it
a try? See if it works for you. Why did breast-feeding have
to be shrouded in warnings about health dangers from bottle feeding that have nothing to do with life in places with
clean drinking water and public sanitation and health
care—as if most of today's breast-feeding mothers were not
themselves formula-fed? If it's so natural, how come there is
a job called "lactation consultant" that requires twenty-five
hundred hours of formal training? "I lay on that heating
pad for nine months with mastitis behind every blocked
milk duct," my friend Pat said when I told her I was writing about new motherhood. "It was excruciating, and I felt
like a complete failure. Then I found out my mother had
gone through exactly the same thing with three out of the
four of us!" Pat's son had colic for nine months. She would
sit at dinner with him screaming in the Snugli on her chest
as she quietly wept and tried not to throw against the wall

the pasta carbonara her cheerful, attentive husband had whipped up after another big day in the office.

Two discourses competed for the terrain of child raising: "parenting" and "mothering." The discourse of parenting was upbeat and funny and liberal and contemporary. It featured men, lots of men, writing in the aren't-I-adorable mode favored by male freelance writers when they venture into the personal, churning out clever 750-word pieces about coaching their daughter's soccer team, helping with homework, explaining why the dog died. Dads made light of their shortcomings and screwups—*Okay, okay, so I dropped the baby on her head, but now she speaks Chinese!* It was as if they were already trying to impress the marital counselor: *I do too cook! I make pancakes! Fantastic pancakes with blueberry smiley faces!* Parenting, as the term implies, expressed the view that mothers and fathers were equally involved in taking care of children.

The discourse of parenting was mostly baloney. Anyone with eyes in her head could see that mothers were still doing most of the work. For example, as the ads for breast pumps and nursing bras and diet pills made clear, they were the ones who read child-care magazines. Parenting made life much more complicated, too, because every decision had to be a joint one even though it was mostly you, the mother, who would be carrying it out. *If she naps now will she stay up too late? How many eggs a week is too many? Jacket or sweater? We agreed you'd try to feed her earlier, remember? We talked about that!* Still, the parenting mode served one very important purpose: it protected you, a little bit, from

the discourse of mothering, which was the ancient and fero-
cious and scornful voice in your head. Right now, that voice
said, you are probably doing something selfish and heedless
and lazy that is placing your child *at risk*, like hiring a sitter
without checking her out with the FBI. Did you even look
at the sell-by date on that salt-laden puree of chemicals you're
spooning into that poor innocent? In the world of mothering, children were always being injured in freak accidents or
getting kidnapped because you zoned out in the park—just
for a moment, but that was all it took. It was the mothering
voice telling women their sons would take drugs and their
daughters would hate them that made women so insecure,
so worried, so hard on themselves. Was it the fault of Freud,
who made infancy so crucial and blamed mothers for invariably screwing it up, as if the least little mistake could warp
a child for life? Was it the lack of simple social rules, lines
of authority, knowable futures? It wasn't as if we were raising our children to work beside us on the farm anymore.
You could be ruining your child now for a way of life that
doesn't even exist yet. There was only one good thing about
the mothering voice: it acknowledged that it was you, the
mother, who was doing the heavy lifting. *Pancakes with
blueberry smiley faces, ha!* the voice cackled. *Isn't that special.* In theory the voice might someday tell you that you
had done a good job after all. When your son got out of
rehab and your daughter had her own kids and started hearing the voice herself.

Meanwhile I held Sophie in my arms and danced around
the living room to Bob Wills and His Texas Playboys. The

winter sun poured in through the white curtains onto my grandmother's faded carpet, and I would think: I am having the most intense experience of my life, and I am having it alone. When Sophie was older and could talk, she would always stop me from singing her to sleep with the one Bob Wills song I knew by heart, my favorite, "There's No Disappointment in Heaven." "No, no," she'd pipe up dreamily, "not that one," and I don't blame her. The words say there's no disappointment, but the music is all disappointment, the sweet, weary, defeated music of sad old wrinkled country people who've worked hard all their lives and are shuffling around a church-basement dance floor, waiting to die. "Sounds of the midnight melt in my ear," I would sing instead. "I know that my beautiful screamer is here."

~

When Sophie started walking, I discovered the playground at West Ninety-first Street, down in Riverside Park. At first I thought it was heaven, with its green painted benches set among big old sycamores and simple, basic equipment out of my own childhood—seesaws, swings, slides, jungle gym, sandbox. I loved its shadiness, its sense of safety, its nothing-special similarity to other playgrounds. I even loved how run-down it was—the scraggly nondescript bushes in the corners, the uneven hexagonal cement pavers, the plain pipe sprinkler that sent the children mad with joy in the heat. The playground belonged to the old Spaldeen-and-egg-cream New York I'd grown up in, in which kids roamed the neighborhood by themselves and read comics in the candy store and getting into Bronx Science made you a genius for sure. It had probably looked much the same in 1950, or even 1920.

After I had been there for a while, the playground seemed less like a delightful municipal bower and more like mommy purdah. How far away the wide, green promenade looked, just beyond the iron fence, where the kidnappers and molesters sauntered by the shimmering Hudson. The playground was the flip side of the post office, the prettier face of exclusion. The only time you saw men there was on the weekends, when businessmen and lawyers and journalists bustled about energetically. The tip-off came when they were leaving and had to collect the toys. "Is this your pail? Come on, Justin, which shovel is yours, this yellow one?" Fakers! It was like Woody Allen wanting custody and not even knowing the names of his son's teachers. The women in the playground watched every move and exchanged knowing half-smiles. All week long, when the playground was theirs again, they traded war stories about manly ineptitude and obliviousness. *Dave went out for Pampers and we didn't see him for weeks! Rick dressed Jenny in the dachshund's coat!* Then they would give a little laugh and roll their eyes because what could they do? They were stuck in it now.

I knew people without children who talked about having a baby to keep their marriage together. Were they insane? You might as well set your house on fire because you were tired of your furniture. Now you *really* had problems. Baby care soaked up all the fun time—was it possible that my husband had ever made me laugh so hard I gasped for breath? That we had made dinner together side by side in our tiny kitchen that now seemed too cramped and narrow for even just me? It obliterated the in-between time too—the moments you spent wondering what Rock Cornish game hens actually were and whether socialism just expected too much of human beings—at the same time that it introduced new arenas of competition: for attention, for sleep, for worktime, for who would get to go to the store for milk or cat food, a prize job because you got to take a walk and be alone for a good half hour. And for a lot of couples, ones who thought they were modern and egalitarian because they had jobs, low standards of cleanliness, and enough money to eat out or order in whenever they wanted, having a baby meant becoming gender Republicans. The old assumptions about men and women, which had been lulled by money and leisure and youthful bohemianism and feminism, woke up. Suddenly it mattered that his job was the one with health insurance, that he made a lot more money, that when you came right down to it he simply was not going to modify whatever his purpose in life had been until now. Just as it mattered that you were the arty freelance one, the bored and restless one, the one who had wanted a baby more. Differences that had seemed like accidents, that could easily have gone the other way, now looked as if they had always been part of the plan. Women spent a lot of time persuading themselves that becoming a gender Republican was natural, but what they meant was that it was inevitable, it was overdetermined, like the First World War. You might as well acquire the frame of mind that justified the reality you had to live with. The alternative was to watch your life recede like a train, winking its red and blue lights. "How old are you?" my friend Dan asked when I raved on enviously about another writer as we watched our daughters totter about the sandbox. "Thirty-seven, thirty-eight? After you turn forty, you won't care."

~

As I watched myself turn into a competent, bland person with a mind furnished by Pottery Barn, the neighborhood was changing in exactly the same way. When we moved to the Upper West Side it was still possible to believe it was not just a haven for wealthy professionals drawn by the big, solid, thick-walled apartments so prized by musicians and, even more, their neighbors. Our building had character— and characters, too, people who'd lived there forever: an old Finnish sailor who exercised in the winter months by walking up and down the stairwell, an ancient woman and her almost equally ancient son who collected trash and stored it in their apartment, the widow of Johnny Pineapple the Hawaiian singer, a pair of left-wing lawyers, a cartoonist. But these people were on the way out; when they died or moved away, the Wall Streeters and corporate lawyers and glossy media types moved in. The mothers in the playground were mostly the new people, clean-living and aggressively pleasant, hardly New Yorkers at all, really. They applied to motherhood the organizational skills that had served them so well in their jobs at Goldman Sachs and

Merrill Lynch—jobs they would never admit they missed, yet that had provided scope for energies that now boiled over within them. They were always arranging holiday parades and mini-camps and finger-painting sessions, and shooing out of the playground the teenagers who liked to fool around on the swings after school, or perhaps instead of school.

To these women, it was clear that the playground would not do. Within months of my arrival there, they had formed a committee to redesign it. The leggy old sycamores would be replaced by tidy islands of greenery; instead of the battered iron equipment—dangerous! uncreative!—there would be elaborate wooden bridge-and-fort combinations, cushioned by rubber mats. The ugly pipe sprinkler would go, too; water would play from fanciful hippopotamus statues. The renovation would be funded by the parks department, with plentiful donations from the corporations for which the mothers had worked, and it would look like a playground in Paris or an old-fashioned children's book. Everything about the proposal irritated me: the fussy design—where was the open space for the kids to run and shriek and play wild games?—the corporate money, those cutesy hippos. The whole thing seemed like a grown-ups' idea of childhood: saccharine, conventional, and channeled. While the mothers bustled about with their blueprints and consultants, I sat with my playground friend Karen, a former social worker whose current stated goal in life was to raise her son to be as little like his ambitious workaholic real-estate-developer father as possible. We joked about asking the committee to install a bar; we even daydreamed about trying to stop the whole project. It just didn't feel democratic, these rich newcomers seizing control of public land and public money to make a fancy little corner for their own fancy children.

Karen and I went to one meeting of the mothers' group, where our concerns about democracy were received with polite bewilderment; everyone else was thrilled that somebody was taking the dirty old playground in hand. In a masterstroke of political maneuvering, the mothers invited us to serve on the committee, an offer that, like the useless malcontents and complainers we were, we evaded. In the end they wrote up a public declaration and got enough signatures to make it look as if they had a lot of community support. Maybe they did. Karen and I sat on our bench by the slide and grumbled, because what, after all, could we do? How can you say to a community board, I love the old sprinkler because it reminds me of myself?

The mothers' committee got their playground, and I had to admit it was darling. In the end, you couldn't even say the project was selfish and elitist, either, because the city fixed up the Ninety-seventh Street playground too, with colorful dinosaur statues for the black and Hispanic kids in that neighborhood to climb on; they even made another animal playground farther north, with dolphins. It's hard for me even to understand, today, what bothered me so much. Maybe I just liked the old neighborhood, which wasn't always making such a production out of everything. Or maybe I liked the old playground because its gray, run-down plainness mirrored my own state of mind. It was a place where you could think your own thoughts, without being jollied along by whimsical sculptures. But by the time they had cut down the sycamores and torn up the old paving stones, I was out of the playground and out of my marriage too.

～

Sophie went to a parent–co-op preschool left over from the neighborhood's radical days. The children celebrated Kwanzaa and Tet; they played Hot Potato and dress-up and learned about Martin Luther King and recycling. I took a part-time editing job. Who knew there could be such exhilaration in catching the subway downtown, buying coffee from a street cart, saying hi to the receptionist? My husband and I shared custody, and never consulted the thick separation agreement our lawyers spent thousands of our dollars squabbling over. On the days Sophie was with me, I did everything exactly the way I wanted. This turned out to be pretty much the way I had been doing things all along, but it felt completely different now that no one was watching me do it. I would read her *Scuffy the Tugboat* and sing "Kevin Barry" as my father had sung it to me, and when she had fallen asleep I would go into my room and lie down on the bed I had shared with my husband, a good man who had done me no wrong. I would smoke a lot of cigarettes and read late into the night like a teenager. When my eyes began to close I would turn on the television and watch Korean costume dramas on a channel somewhere on the edge of cable. Trapped in the little box, women in stiff, elaborate red-and-gold gowns stalked back and forth before thrones and altars and occasionally even whole armies, declaiming, exhorting, berating, bewailing in voices as high and harsh as those of cats in heat.

Despite the lack of subtitles, I understood every word.

GOOD-BYE, LENIN

I HADN'T PLANNED TO BUY A BOX—OR, AS IT IS called in the funeral business, casket—for my father's ashes, or, as they are called, cremains. I thought I would just use the container they came back in. I had read my Jessica Mitford, I knew all about how undertakers jack up prices to take advantage of your grief and inexperience; it's not as though you've done a lot of comparison shopping or can hold off until a good sale comes along. I briefly considered a ceramic canister in the window of the trendy housewares store that had opened on Atlantic Avenue around the corner from my father's house. It had a pattern of emerald-green dragonflies floating on a deep blue glaze, and every time I passed by on my way to visit my father in the two weeks he lay in his death coma in the stroke ward of Long Island

Hospital I went through the same internal dialogue: I want that / it costs fifty dollars and you have nothing to put in it / *How can you think of tchotchkes at a time like this?* Now I had something to put in it, but I could just hear my father protesting this blow to his manly pride from the afterlife that neither of us believed in. *Dragonflies?* To be turned into cremains was bad enough—it sounded like off-brand cat food—but to take one's final rest in a fancified candy jar would be just too much. On the other hand, the surprisingly heavy plastic box of grit and gravel I eventually received reminded me of leftovers forgotten in the back of the fridge. Gray shadowy lumps rattled around in there. I'm not one of these people who are obsessed by the proper disposition of the dead—if I died in an explosion or a plane crash I wouldn't want people knocking themselves out hunting down bits of me and distinguishing them from other people's bits. But still. I wouldn't want to spend eternity in Tupperware either, even thought there would be no "I" to know or care.

"There's no rush," said Charlie, the undertaker, with a world-weary wave of the hand. "You can always come back and choose something later." A surprising number of relatives, he had told me, never return for the cremains at all, so to him I was already a dutiful, if indecisive, daughter who would, in the end, want to do the right thing. Charlie was the old Brooklyn—hugely obese, sweaty, mustached, and balding. His funeral parlor was the old Brooklyn too: its murals of roses and trellises by an improbably turquoise sea gave it the look of a neighborhood Italian restaurant—one of the old-fashioned veal-and-spaghetti places that were being driven out of business by the hip new bistros for the hip new people. Within minutes of meeting me, Charlie had congratulated me on avoiding his competitor, who was rumored to be associated with the Mafia and to cremate bodies in batches and hand back any old shovelful to the family, and moved on to the tale of how his Egyptian grandmother met his grandfather, a Maltese sailor. It was a good story, but perhaps because my father had died only hours before I don't remember anything about it. I lugged the box back to my father's house and stashed it in the upstairs hall closet while I figured out what to do with it.

"You should write about the death of the second parent," a friend suggested recently. "What it's like to feel like no one is ahead of you in line." Yes, that is what it feels like; you have lost your shield, you are definitely next. "I'm an orphan," my sixty-year-old father had said only half mock-tragically when his mother had died at eighty-four. He'd sounded surprised, too, to feel that cold wind. The dead relatives don't go away, though: they're behind you, around you, just out of sight. It's as if as parents and grandparents and aunts and uncles die you acquire over time, person by person, a silent, invisible family just like the one you had before, only now, if you are lucky, they are entirely benevolent and full of wisdom. It's easy to see how primitive peoples worship their dead relatives. The things they leave behind glow with power and mystery, like the objects in a cargo cult.

For a while I thought I would move into my father's

house, which was now mine, and where I had grown up. I could make Martinson's Red in the old drip coffeepot, reread the beautiful Heritage Book Club editions of *A Connecticut Yankee* and *Les Misérables*, and pick up where I had left off at fifteen in the *Marxist Handbook*, which my mother had won for selling the most subscriptions to the *Daily Worker* in 1947. I could sleep in my old bedroom, where my white lace high-school graduation dress still hung in the closet, and work in my father's study, still painted a pale 1950s-classroom green and lit by one of those plain fluorescent standing lamps detectives open their mail by in film noirs. People used to live all their lives in the houses they grew up in. Nobody thought it was strange.

I couldn't sleep there a single night. My parents were everywhere—listening to Paul Robeson on the worn living room couch, kissing in the kitchen, sulking and fighting, drinking, dying. At any moment I expected to hear my father's smoker's cough, a loud horrible strangled sound he never bothered to muffle. I could practically see in the corner of their bedroom the can of Coke my mother had tossed aside the night her liver failed twenty-six years ago, and feel again how that had seemed to embody the loneliness and unknowableness of her life. The liver and kidneys shutting down would have made her thirsty and nauseated, but she would not have known that. She would have thought, I'll just get into bed with a cold soda. In the end, I spent three days cleaning and tidying and making bundles of my father's clothes to give away, left a note for the new tenants, and fled.

But first, I went down into the basement and looked through my father's file cabinets. There were six of these, with five drawers each, organized with lawyerly carefulness. As if he had known I would come looking, there was a black-and-white marbled composition book in the uppermost drawer of the farthest cabinet listing the contents of all the other drawers. Everything was where he had noted it would be: financial records, his own and those of clients, going back thirty years; paperwork on the house, the car, insurance, my mother's will. There were drawers for the estates of which he had been executor: Mrs. Balsam, who had taught art at my high school, ancient Mrs. Gill across the street, who lived in total squalor in the basement of her trash-filled brownstone and had to have her foot, and then her leg, amputated because of neglected diabetes; my father said it was Mrs. Gill who made him see that some people just don't care if they wake up in the morning or not. There were three drawers crammed with research into family history—the Midsouth preachers and teachers of his grandparents' generation, and his once-famous great-uncle, Elbert Hubbard, who wrote "A Message to Garcia" and went down on the *Lusitania*. My father was always trying to get me interested in my ancestors—for example, my grandmother's British grandfather, Happy Jack Olarenshaw, who had run away from home after he dropped his baby brother Moses Henry on his head, joined Queen Victoria's army, fought in India, and ended his days as a street evangelist in Cincinnati. He was said to have converted many solid citizens, including Procter, or possibly Gamble, by approaching them at two and three in the morning as they were making their way home from the red-light district feeling low and sinful. Except for Happy Jack, I never could keep those people straight or remember how I was related to them. My parents were about as much family history as I could take.

~

It wasn't until I was in college that my parents actually said in so many words that they had belonged to the Communist Party. This wasn't a secret, exactly, they probably would have told me if I had asked. But McCarthy-era habits of caution were deeply ingrained, even in me; I had never asked them directly. Still, long before my mother told a funny story about going to pick up her lost wallet at the police station—and was her face red, because her party card was inside with her charge-a-plates from A&S and Martin's—I had figured it out. I knew why my father couldn't work for the federal government like his mother and his uncle George, and I knew why on the way home from Jones Beach on summer evenings he rolled up the windows of the car before he broke into "The Internationale," "Whirlwinds of Danger," "Banks of Marble," or "Long-Haired Preachers," brave old songs that make my eyes tear even now. My parents had friends who had been fired, blacklisted, arrested. Abe, who had been disbarred, ghost-wrote briefs for other lawyers. Judy had been tried as a spy. On our living room wall hung a cheerful watercolor of a field of sunflowers that Arnold had painted in prison. Once two beefy FBI agents came to the house and my mother closed the door in their faces. "I don't have to talk to you," she told them in a tight, level voice, "and I'm not going to." We watched through the dining room window as they lifted the lids on our garbage cans outside and poked around inside like demented chefs, just to show that they could.

By today's standards of educated middle-class child raising, I should be traumatized. What, they let you think they might be *arrested*? No wonder you were always sleepwalking into their bed! But although there must have been moments when my parents were worried, perhaps truly frightened, my father presented the difficulties of the McCarthy era as the latest chapter in the exciting story of workers versus the ruling class, good versus evil, right versus wrong—the great trajectory of history. You couldn't escape it, even if you wanted to. Take my elderly fussbudgety kindergarten teacher, Mrs. Meeker. She seemed nice enough, my father admitted, but deep down she was on the side of the bosses. Sure enough, a few weeks later Mrs. Meeker made me pick up and eat a turkey slice I had discreetly let slip to the lunchroom floor because the peas next to it had turned it green. If she had been on the workers' side, she would never have done that; she would have understood that if turkey was green, it might have been poisoned, and that children should not have to eat food that frightened them.

My mother and most of my parents' political friends were Jewish, but being a radical—that was the word they used—seemed to me like being a particularly dashing kind of Christian: you fought poverty and injustice, even if the bosses martyred you like Sacco and Vanzetti and the

Rosenbergs, and you wrestled for souls, like Happy Jack. If Cousin Arthur called us only from pay phones because he thought our phone was tapped, that just showed what kind of person he was. The things that mattered to the world— money, fame, status—were not the important things. In fact, if you had too much of them you had probably *sold out.* There was a secret history behind the visible one, and in that hidden, truer version of events the last might be first, as it said in the Bible, and the nobody might be the hero, like the Scarlet Pimpernel as played by Leslie Howard on *Million Dollar Movie,* except he was on the wrong side.

"See that man over there?" my father said one day when we were having lunch at Armando's. He nodded toward a huge white-haired, red-faced man in a rumpled suit a few tables over. "He was going to assassinate Hitler." History's wing could brush past while you were spooning your bisque tortoni from its pleated paper cup. On the other hand, *going to?* They sent him all the way to Germany, but, what, something came up? Communists gave a lot of credit for intention, which was strange, because if the course of history was inevitable, as Karl Marx held it to be, your intentions, good or bad, would not make much of a difference, any more than the thoughts of a mountain climber matter to an avalanche. All that would matter was that you did the right thing from history's point of view. Communism's obsession with thoughts—the right analysis, the right line—was another way in which it was like Christianity. A moral drama was going on inside you, and someone—God, the Party, History—was watching every minute. "You have been weighed in the balance and found wanting." For years this verse from the Bible gave me a scary thrill. It meant records were being kept, as in some celestial file cabinet. You could be called to account at any moment, and when that moment came you could be Leslie Howard or you could be Cousin Arthur.

Which side would I be on? Maybe the test had come without my knowing and I had already failed. Maybe it would never come, and I would never truly know myself. Or maybe it would come, but the right answer would also be the wrong answer: the result would be not glory but obscurity. This seemed entirely likely. There were a few Communists who had managed to trump their adversaries publicly—Georgi Dimitroff, for example, who had argued so fiercely and cleverly when he was charged with setting the Reichstag fire that the Nazis themselves had had to acquit him. Now, there was a hero for you! But mostly, in my family, heroism was of a peculiar, negative sort. It meant silence: not naming names, not giving information, not talking to the FBI, not signing a loyalty oath, not selling out. It was bound up with concepts like honor and conscience and nobility and the romance of failure, like Athos, the melancholy representative of the dying feudal order, who was the Musketeer I most wanted to be. Or the wastrel (romantic word!) Sydney Carton, from *A Tale of Two Cities*, who redeemed himself by taking his best friend's place on the scaffold, and whom my friends in the eighth grade all thought my father much resembled when he came to school on Father-Daughter Day, tall and handsome in his blue-and-white-striped seersucker suit from Brooks Brothers.

Naturally, as a child I agreed with my parents. I knew *Mad* magazine's "Spy vs. Spy" cartoon was reactionary because it was drawn by an émigré from Castro's Cuba—a *gusano*—and portrayed the Cold War as an amoral battle of wits. I knew *Animal Farm* was Trotskyite propaganda, although I didn't know what a Trotskyite was or why we didn't call them Trotskyists. When we sang "Avanti popolo" around the piano at the Behrstocks' Christmas party, I was proud when I heard my father's voice singing not "*evviva il socialismo e la libertà*" but "*communismo.*" Socialists like the Behrstocks just didn't get it.

In high school I began to separate myself. "Hungarians!" my father would snort if over dinner I brought up the suppression of the Hungarian revolution of 1956. "You mean, the Fascists? Hungary had the first Fascist dictatorship in Europe. It was allied with Hitler, for God's sake." Before I could think of a comeback, he followed up with a brief history of Hungary, giving special attention to its anti-Semitism, feudal backwardness, and long-standing desire to dominate Poland—"Remember, it was the Austro-*Hungarian* Empire"—moving right along to the sufferings the Soviet Union nobly endured to free the Hungarians from the Nazis, whom most of them were more than happy to accommodate. "Socialism," he would finish triumphantly—because, confusingly, Communists called communism socialism, while despising the milquetoasty Socialists—"was too good for them." There I was, defending Hitler's best friends. The same thing happened if I argued that the Soviet Union had unjustly invaded Finland (more best friends of Hitler), kept half of it (reparations), and forced itself on Eastern Europe (protection from Western aggression, and who won the Second World War anyway? Not Czechoslovakia!). If feminism hadn't come along on its high horse, I would never have won an argument in that house.

Like a lot of lawyers in the party, my father combined uncritical devotion to the imaginary Soviet Union in his head with a passion for rights and the Constitution straight out of the ACLU charter. If you want to be cynical about it, you could say their commitment to civil liberties was just a self-serving tactic, but I think it was more that their minds ran on parallel tracks and they believed what they believed while they were believing it. They were like Christians who put their faith in both miracles and surgery. One minute my father would be dismissing the Gulag with clichés like "History is written in blood" and "You can't make an omelet without breaking eggs." The next, he'd be expatiating on the humane wisdom of the American legal code, in which attempted murder was punished more lightly than murder, because even if it looked like your intention was exactly the same in each case, maybe your aim was that little bit off or you didn't put in quite enough poison because your conscience deflected your hand. He could justify the forced collectivization of the kulaks between two bites of a baked potato—not that reports of mass starvation were anything but anti-Soviet propaganda, like the Moscow show trials, so called.

But the sorrows of his clients got to him. "Don't answer," my mother would say when the phone in the hall rang yet again at dinnertime. "It's Phoebe." It was amazing how accurately my mother could predict which of my father's needy, irritating clients was invading our family time. Phoebe was a mentally troubled woman who had lost her baby to the social workers and wanted my father to get her visitation with her now eight-year-old son. He always went to the phone, and we'd hear him patiently explaining something boring and complicated as Phoebe threw an inaudible tantrum on the other end and our food got cold, because this was the patriarchal age when eating started and stopped with the father. I hated Phoebe, for ruining dinner and annoying my mother and inflicting herself on that little boy and his new parents—those good, rescuing, innocent, sane parents!—just to make a point. Sure enough, my father won her case, but she never did contact her son. All that suffering and anxiety and disruption for nothing! I doubt she even paid him. "She was too destroyed," he said sadly when I said, *You see?* "Too ashamed." And the thing was, he was right: the social workers *had* stolen crazy Phoebe's baby.

There was another reason I hated Phoebe, though. My father was so obviously too good for her: He should be defending selfless revolutionaries, I thought, not promoting the dim fantasies of lost souls. That he didn't seem to mind— that he was courteous to Phoebe, no matter how hungry he was and how cold dinner got, and not only wouldn't tell her not to bother us at night but seemed to find her legal problems interesting and significant—exasperated me. And Phoebe wasn't the only client who seemed to me drenched in futility. There was Ben Meyers, an adman who had quit his job and left his wife and children to move to Greenwich Village and paint, only to drop dead of a heart attack almost immediately. My father's connection with Ben Meyers was entirely posthumous; he handled the estate, which consisted mostly of awful artwork—hulking nudes, muddy abstracts, woodcuts that looked as if they been hacked out of moldy logs with a steak knife. But even though he couldn't get to a phone, Ben Meyers bothered me almost as much as Phoebe. I saw him as a failure who had ruined his family for nothing. What was the point of devoting your life to Art if you had no talent? But my father thought it was good that Ben Meyers had followed his 40-watt star. "He had something," my father would say, even if he couldn't get it down in paint. When he couldn't find a friend or relative of Meyers's who wanted his pictures, he stacked them in the basement, where they remained for years. Well, you couldn't just throw them out. Possibly they disintegrated in one of the many floods that plagued the cellar, because by my father's later years only a single watercolor remained to mark Ben Meyers's existence, an abstract of brownish-black vaguely fecal shapes obscuring a multicolored background. To me the painting was so depressing, such an obvious representation of blockage and muddle, I was surprised when my father framed it and hung it in the downstairs hallway. He said it reminded him of the old-fashioned cast-iron stoves of his childhood—how you could look inside and see red and blue and gold flames playing among the coals.

⌒

By bourgeois standards my father was not a big success in solo practice. He wasn't very litigious, for one thing: he was always trying to get his divorce clients to give their marriage another try. He wasn't much of a businessman either. "You don't have to make every dollar in the world," he'd tell me during the years the dissident painters trooped in and out of the house in their endless struggle to get the mob out of their union. Still, perhaps he wondered, as I did, if this was what the revolution was about. He spent a lot of time in the garden, which was always in the process of some big transformation that never quite took off: summersweet bushes that never became a "living fence" as the catalog promised, a fountain that was supposed to run on solar power, and maybe would have in the Gobi Desert. He took up projects: learning to sail, a chemistry class at the New School. We made wine from dandelions that we harvested at dawn in Prospect Park. Six months later our big glass jug was full of a beautiful translucent golden liquid that tasted like rotten hay. These innocent projects filled me with anxiety. Would Georgi Dimitroff have been so proud of his A in chemistry that he laminated his report card? I blushed for shame when my father's secondhand Sunfish sank in Lake Mahopac as my mother's mother looked on with pursed lips. I forgot that just a few days before, he had sailed me in that same contraption to the uninhabited island in the center of the lake, a place I had longed to visit since I was four, and we had walked all over it and found an old stone wall, standing, as mysterious as the statues on Easter Island, in the middle of the oaks and maples.

Still, his career had its moments. Somewhere in the basement, I remembered from years ago, was a cardboard box containing the records of *Killian v. United States,* my father's one Supreme Court case. He worked on it for years. James Killian was a United Autoworkers official who, according to the government, lied when he affirmed in an affidavit that he was not a member of the Communist Party; for this, he had been sentenced to five years in prison for perjury. The FBI's informers testified that they had seen Killian at party meetings. Among other points, my father argued that their testimony was invalid because they had not retained their notes and the Bureau had relied on their oral reports, given later, instead. That seemed like a pretty good argument to me—memory can play tricks on anyone. When the great day came, in 1961, he was so nervous he wouldn't let my mother and me come to Washington to hear him, but we took the train down anyway and sat quietly in the back of the courtroom, where he wouldn't see us. We were so proud of him! And he must have been glad in the end that we were there, because there's a picture of us standing on the Supreme Court steps, my mother smiling and elegant in her wool suit from Peck & Peck, me for once not wearing a vacant scowl. When the decision came down months later, the Court went against him six to three. Felix Frankfurter may have tried to save the Rosenbergs, but he sold my father out. He was a lackey of the ruling class after all.

"Almost everything is evidence of something," said the Court in its oracular way, "but that does not mean nothing can ever safely be destroyed." Oh, but it does. That is exactly what it means. If everything is evidence of something, then nothing can ever safely be destroyed. I know this because after my father's death I spent hours in that dark filthy cellar, rummaging through those file cabinets and the cracked plaid suitcases and the cardboard boxes full of old Christmas cards and broken gadgets. I even went back one weekend when the tenants were away and searched through the whole place again. But I was never able to find that box of papers from the Killian case, proof of my father's glory, which had lit my adolescence with its underground glow.

~

What I did find, preserved in the original postal carton in which he had received it in 1984, thanks to the Freedom of Information Act, was my father's FBI file. It was about five inches thick and impressively censored; whole paragraphs, even a few whole pages, were blacked out. A lot of people must have been informing on him, going all the way back to someone at Western High School in Washington, D.C. ("he became actively engaged in Communism and made numerous communist speeches from 'Soap Boxes' "); a college classmate ("if POLLITT had had to make a choice between the United States and Russia at the time he attended Harvard, he was quite convinced POLLITT would be on the side of Moscow"); and a "Washington newspaper executive" who told FBI agent Mary Spargo in 1941 that he'd heard my father was a Communist from the father of my father's then girlfriend, who herself unwittingly informed on him when she shared a room with Mary Spargo at the American People's Meeting in New York. As a result of these and other tidbits, my father, twenty-one years old, lost his job clerking in the War Department, where he was a founding member of the oddly titled War Department Peace Club, and later was bounced from the Air Cadet Corps and reduced to a private.

I learned some interesting things about my father from his file. I learned that his IQ was 132 and that the tag beneath his high-school senior yearbook photo was "He says that he is a radical and not the least bit interested in the opposite sex." I learned that he lost his scholarship to Harvard for "making communistic speeches and engaging in communistic activities" as a seventeen-year-old freshman. I learned that he had been arrested in Watertown on August 7, 1939, or possibly April, or maybe January 1937, for "distributing handbills without a permit in connection with the rubber workers union." I learned that he took courses in "political theory, which was a study of Althusius, Locke, Hobbes, Rousseou, Marx and Heggel." (Althusius?) I learned that he stated on his civil service application that he had taken a course in the economics of socialism, "which dealt exclusively with the Economic Principles of Carl Marx, Founder of Communism and criticisms thereof" and that he told Mary Spargo, in an official interview, that the Communist Party "had a legitimate place in the United States labor movement." That's telling her, Dad!

His finest moment came in 1950. By now married, a lawyer, and a father, he agreed to meet with two agents for a confidential discussion of an unidentified woman. He showed up with a lawyer and told the agents he "considered this my right." When they said they would have to cancel

the interview he replied that he would like to make a statement. He said he was opposed to the loyalty program and its
"policy of guilt by association" and would not admit to
knowing the woman in question because even if he only
knew her slightly and said so she would be considered guilty
since "you fellows, no doubt, have a file on me." This incident reverberates through his files for decades—the Bureau
just couldn't get over it. You fellows! The Scarlet Pimpernel
couldn't have put it with more flair. The agents were still
going on about it in 1963 ("in view of the foregoing, it is felt
that recontact of subject would prove unproductive and possibly result in embarrassment to the Bureau").

Given its resources, the FBI seemed to have a curiously
hard time getting my father in its sights. It took agents from
1948 to 1951 to establish the date of his birth; even longer
to figure out that "Basil Pollitt" and "Basil R. Pollitt" were
not "aliases" of Basil Riddiford Pollitt—whereupon they
promptly added Basil H. Pollitt, his father, to his alias list,
along with the assorted misspellings our last name seems to
attract. They listed his height as five foot eight and five foot
ten. They mistook him for his brother and sent him off to
France. Their flat-footed bureaucratic diction put sinister
constructions on mysteries that were the result of their own
mistakes—those many "aliases," their inability to find my
father's birth certificate, as if his claim to have been born in
Huntington, West Virginia, was some clever Communist
trick. They made "pretext" calls to the house to verify his
address and spoke to "an unidentified female who professed
to be the wife of the subject" and "a male, professing to be

the subject." Right, maybe some *other* wily Communists had picked up the phone. Still, in the file they referred to *Killian v. United States* as "a celebrated case." Even now, it makes me happy that they recognized his worth.

~

What did the FBI know about my father? Most of what they listed was in the public record. He belonged to a lot of organizations—the American Labor Party, the National Lawyers Guild, of which he was a board member, the Fair Play for Cuba Committee—some of them close to the party, all of them legal. He worked on the defense of party leaders in various Smith Act cases, and he was a staff lawyer for the United Electrical Workers, a Communist-dominated union. Beyond that, they couldn't seem to get him in focus. On September 23, 1954, they observed him "in the company of ROSS RUSSELL and two other men leave UE headquarters at 11 E 51st Street, New York City. The four men had lunch together and then returned to UE headquarters"; On the evening of April 29, 1955, an agent "observed BASIL POL-LITT on the fringe of the crowd gathered at Union Square, New York City, for the May Day demonstration." Despite "intensive efforts" and use of a concealed camera "under such condition as to preclude any possibility of embarrassment to the Bureau which might arise from the subjects employment as an attorney and his connection with the NLG"—the National Lawyers Guild—it took them six months to get a photo of him. ("He is observed only infrequently because of his employment at his residence.") When they finally caught him on film, the pictures proved "not a good likeness of the subject." Fussy, fussy! It took them another year to get one they approved of. ("Excellent"!) It's as if capturing his image had consumed the original purpose of the investigation, because once they had their photo, they had little more to say. Or maybe the purpose of the investigation was simply to provide employment for FBI agents. They closed his file in 1971. At least, that's their story. It was a joke on the Left that if you requested your file, they immediately started one, just as my father had said back in 1950. Perhaps the file I was reading was a decoy and they continued to make their annual pretext phone call and trail him at a discreet distance around the neighborhood. Maybe they noted his presence at anti-war marches through the 1970s and into the 1980s; looked over the briefs, in which he argued, unsuccessfully but presciently, that grand juries were unconstitutional because they systematically excluded blacks and women; read the letters he sent over the years to the *New York Times* and *Harvard Magazine;* sat behind him at Alger Hiss's funeral in 1996. "It was a good turnout," he told me, as though reporting on a demonstration. "But it didn't have any politics. Nobody talked about the case."

~

Here are some things the FBI didn't know: In 1960, when Fidel—we always called him by his first name at our house—came to New York, my father went up to the Hotel Theresa in Harlem to be in the welcoming crowd. In 1966, he and my mother sent me on a Quaker youth trip to the

Soviet Union, where I was French-kissed by a French boy and did my bit for coexistence by trading my extra pair of blue jeans to a Leningrad girl named Alla in return for a recording of Prokofiev's *War and Peace.* In 1973, driving through Manhattan on the way to my aunt's for Thanksgiving, my father saw a black teenager being splayed against a car by a white policeman. He parked, dashed out, and I could see him having a dramatic conversation with the officer. "I wanted him to know a lawyer was watching," he said when he got back in the car. He never left the party, even after he heretically sided with China in the Sino-Soviet split. The party simply fell apart around him.

Here are some other things: He knew the words to hundreds of forgotten popular songs—"My Gal's a Corker," "I Had a Hat When I Came In," "A Bird in a Gilded Cage"—and all the verses of "Ivan Skavinsky Skivar." He called Italians eye-ties and wops and dagos. He told me not to become a lawyer because the law was coarsening. He told me men are the makers of civilization and women are its bearers. He woke me for school every morning with a quatrain from the *Rubáiyát*—"Wake! For the Sun who scatter'd into flight / The Stars before him from the Field of Night / Drives Night along with them from Heav'n and strikes / The Sultán's Turret with a Shaft of Light." This never failed to irritate me, but now I wonder if any child on earth is roused from sleep like that. After my mother died he turned my bedroom into an off-the-books bed-and-breakfast and, despite being an atheist, prominently displayed on my old bureau a framed biblical verse in needlepoint about entertaining angels unawares. He kept a small bust of Lenin on a bookshelf and a photograph of Paul Robeson on the living room wall, but he voted for Giuliani after a black rioter killed a Jew in Crown Heights. He even, in the end, made money, like a lot of Communists. All those years of scrutinizing the economy for signs of imminent collapse taught them something. He was eighty when he told me, "Basically I wake up every day with a song in my heart." Around the same age as when he said, "I've seen a lot of broken eggs, but I never saw that damn omelet."

~

In the end I put the plastic box in a shopping bag and lugged it over to Charlie's. "I thought you'd be back," he said. I picked out a casket that was stout and solid and covered in bright red lacquer; it looked cheerful and sturdy and vaguely Chinese. Well, he'd always admired Mao. "Good choice," said Charlie, heaving himself out of his chair to pour my father into his final resting place somewhere discreetly out of sight. As I waited in Charlie's office, I thought it was probably time to think about burying him with my mother, as he had wanted. The cemetery was only for Jews, but maybe I could say he had converted. After all, Marx was Jewish, so there was definitely a connection. I would have to think of something—I had put his house up for sale, and my apartment had only one closet.

I had various ideas about what to write on his headstone. Sometimes I leaned toward another of his favorite verses from the *Rubáiyát:*

Ah love! Could thou and I with Fate conspire
To grasp this sorry Scheme of Things entire,
Would not we shatter it to bits—and then
Re-mould it nearer to the Heart's Desire!

Its romanticism was exciting and theatrical, but also suspect: destroying everything to remake it from scratch hadn't worked out very well in the twentieth century. There was another poem he liked to recite, from a book I'd had as a child:

When I grow up I'll carry a stick
And be very dignified,
I'll have a watch that will really tick,
My house will be tall and built of brick,
And no one will guess it's really a trick,
And I'm myself inside.

Perhaps, since a tombstone has two sides, I could use them both.

Sitting in Charlie's office, I remembered a story my father had told me about coming to New York in 1945. He had walked up Fifth Avenue on a beautiful spring afternoon, feeling bad because he hadn't got out of his four years in the army any of the things he'd wanted. He'd longed to be a pilot, but thanks to the War Department Peace Club and Mary Spargo and the rest, he had been kicked out of flight school. He'd wanted to fight in Europe, but it was all he could do to get shipped to the Pacific; the army hadn't wanted to send him overseas at all. He thought about the wounded men he had helped load onto planes in Saipan and how some of them were probably dead by the time they landed in Hawaii. And then he let it all fall away. The war was over, and he was alive. He went into a Schrafft's and when the waitress came he ordered chocolate ice cream with marshmallow sauce. For the rest of his life, he told me, that was the taste of joy.

END OF

I USED TO LOVE TO GO THE LONG WAY ROUND TO GET to my house in Connecticut. I'd take the right-hand fork off Route 1 at the Shell station and turn onto Beach Park Road, drive past a gaggle of modest ranch-style houses and the Catholic cemetery with its border of dark red maples—meticulously spaced, spookily identical—and suddenly, there it would be, the view that lifted my heart: empty fields stepping off into salt marsh, tidal flats, and, off in the distance, Long Island Sound. It was as if a painter had tried to create a sense of depth using only endless different shades of green: yellow-green close up for the fields near the road, big stripes of vivid emerald and duller jade for the long grass beyond, green-tinged turquoise for the water, a green-black smudge for the line of pines on Cedar Island. All those closely related intensities right up against each other created a kind of dazzle, almost like a mirage or a heat wave.

By next year that view will be gone forever, replaced by the Hammocks, an upscale development for "active adults"—people over fifty-five with no children at home. "Active adults"—do they make you move out if you start lying around the house watching Judge Judy berate some young fool and eating leftover spaghetti straight from the fridge? If you inherit an adorable orphan through an improbable twist of fate, like those grumpy oldsters in made-for-TV movies, too bad. You'll have to take in a wise old homeless person instead. "Hammock" is not a reference to the hanging string bed—that wouldn't fit the active image either; it's a regional variation on "hummock," as in hillock or small hill. The variation's region is Florida, as it happens, which makes it an odd choice for a New England field that was, moreover, entirely flat even before the bulldozers obliterated it. You can see why "the Hummocks" wouldn't work, though—it sounds slovenly and depressing, like a housing project. My neighbor Cindy, who knows everything going on in town, tells me there's nothing to be done. All the towns around here are trying to attract prosperous retirees; they pay taxes and don't use the schools. Moreover, the land was already a single parcel, so it didn't need a lot of permissions and variances from the town council. It belonged to the family that ran the local plant nursery; they used part of it to grow rows of box and juniper and miniature arborvitae, the stiff, spiky bushes people in this part of Connecticut spend their summers pruning into submission. The kids didn't want to be in the garden-center supply business, and who can blame them? It's all the work of farming with none of the moral superiority. The developers could have been worse, too: they worked with the town to protect the wetlands from sewage and to keep the fifty-three houses, what's the word I want—tactful? Right now the raw wood frames rising from the muddy, churned-up earth look as hulking and as out of place as a fleet of stranded Noah's arks, but in ten years, with trees and flowers and all-weather wicker furniture dotting the lawns and colorful holiday banners flapping from the porches, those fifty-three houses will seem as if they've been there for half a century. In twenty years, no one will remember the precise look of that big expanse of green floating down to the water, the sky over it as huge as in a Dutch marine painting. Maybe I won't remember it either—the way I can't remember the look of the woods that stood where they built the sprawling new police station, or which sweet shingled cottage was torn down to build which new gigantic summer home that can't decide whether to be a lighthouse or a French château. I drive the other way now, so I won't see the bulldozers.

The view from Beach Park Road isn't the only thing that's just about finished. My whole adult life I've spent moving into neighborhoods that promptly began demolishing the features that drew me there: delis run by ancient Italian couples who keep a coffee cup full of single cigarettes for sale on the counter, used-book stores, new-book stores, Cuban-Chinese restaurants, movie theaters with Art

Deco facades and only one screen, banks that look like Greek temples, affordable apartments and the people who live in them. This morning, as I was rummaging in the fridge for butter—well, actually, for cholesterol-lowering heart-protective 40-percent-fewer-calories tile grout— *Weekend Edition* informed me that Bengal tigers are disappearing from India. Bengal tigers are the very symbol of India, and there are game parks set up especially for them with everything they like, lots of forest, lots of space, lots of food. I picture them padding about, sleek and powerful, in the filtered green light under the trees. Yet some game parks have no tigers at all anymore; poachers have been taking them. *But why?* the reporter asks in a twinkly voice, as if there is something quaint and faintly absurd about this whole Bengal tiger thing, as if it's some kind of Agatha Christie locked-park wildlife mystery: *The Tiger Vanishes, Ten Little Tigers, Who Killed Roger Tiger?* I feel a surge of hatred that is the closest I ever come to understanding the red states: you prissy, self-satisfied, overeducated jerk, this is all a big joke to you, isn't it? And then I immediately feel guilty, because how can someone ever have too much education? By the time I've taken due note of my covert anti-intellectualism and imagined the reporter dangling limply like a mouse from a tiger's viselike jaws, he's moved on to a story about wacky graduation speakers and I have been staring into space for some time. It's only eight-thirty and I feel like I've been up for hours.

The tiger item took me by surprise, actually. I usually try to avoid stories about the environment: vanishing wildlife, melting glaciers, spreading deserts, strip malls and cul-de-sacs eating up all the beautiful secret places. I feel I know enough already to understand that nature is done for. The details will just make me sad without suggesting anything I can do. Human beings have a chance; we're strong and smart and vicious. Some of us will always survive—five hundred million once global warming really gets going, according to Dr. James Lovelock, who invented the Gaia theory, which always sounded so New Agey and dumb, but who knows? Maybe the earth really is a single organism and can take only so much garbage and abuse before it rebels. Five hundred million people is still a lot more humans than tigers. To say nothing of Adélie penguins. According to a letter to the *New Yorker* from Ron Naveen, a bird specialist who has spent the last twenty-two summers in Antarctica, their population has decreased by half over those years. Things aren't looking good for blue-eyed shags either. Whatever they are. Or, he might have added, the Irrawaddy dolphins of Cambodia or the hedgehogs of Britain or monarch butterflies. "Ultimately," he writes, "it seems that humans are incapable of thinking in time frames exceeding their own life spans." Oh, Ron, it's so much worse than that—because all this destruction and despoilment is happening not in some future we're too stupid to imagine but right now, during our own life spans. Humans have trouble thinking about even ten years from now, when the effects of global warming will be irreversible, if they aren't already, and Bangladeshis will be floating about on rafts like the Atoll Dwellers in *Waterworld*. People have a hard time figuring out whether to order a burger or a BLT, or whether to call now or wait to see if there's a message on the machine at home. Finish the *Times* or watch *Law and Order?* It can take quite a while to decide. By the time people focus on something as vast as the environment and figure out some huge multilateral international coordinated response and get all the enforcement mechanisms up and running, we'll have boiled to death in our beds. Already, you open the paper and there are photos of red and yellow and turquoise frogs that can no longer be found in the Costa Rican rain forest and you never even knew frogs came in those colors.

~

But then, a lot of things seem to be drawing to a close. Type "End of" into the search engine at Amazon.com and up comes a staggering list of nouns: the end of poverty, the end of faith, the end of oil, the end of history, the end of Christendom. To say nothing of blackness, stress, time, the certain world, nature, racism, art, diets, elsewhere, work, marketing, fashion, victory culture, cancer, philosophy, the age, sorrow, eternity, science, advertising, cinema as we know it, homework, the nation state, the European era, the American era, education, celluloid, diversity, reform, software, the game, the Cold War, medicine, globalization, certainty, the American gospel, enterprise, illusions, ideology, democracy, innocence, shareholder value, the art world, equality, the soul, print, privacy, progress, beauty, evolution, the millennium, Utopia, the dream, politics, the novel of love, the twentieth century, the poem, sex, gender, sanity, the republic, magic, religion, logic, agriculture, order, medicine, the rainbow, civilization, boxing, baseball, patience, Detroit, New York, what was, the earth, the world, the story, the road, the line. And don't forget libraries—googling will soon mean the end of those. No more handing in your little slip and breathing in the wonderful warm smell of old bound paper while you wait for your book to come up in the dumbwaiter. It's as if humanity is jettisoning everything too complicated or heavy or fussy or impractical (the novel of love! the poem!) for the single suitcase it can lug into the crowded, stripped-down, functional-dysfunctional future. Already I miss the strong verbs—*shone* and *dove* and *spat*—with their weighty, distinctive, biblical-sounding vowels like a core of darkness, as if their pastness spread outward from their very heart. Even ten years ago you heard them all the time. Now it's *shined*, like a cheap flashlight, and *dived*, which has no depth, while *spit*, for some reason, has lost its past tense entirely.

"America was better when it had more trees and fewer people," my father said the year before he died. As a child in the Depression he had lived all over America, in places that were smaller and prettier than they are now: Coral Gables and Phoenix and Montclair, New Jersey—distinct towns with their own personalities, and centers that you could get to on your bicycle after school without being run over or kidnapped or even having to wear a helmet—and Staten Island, which was practically the country right there in New York Harbor. You're not supposed to say things like that, though; people look at you like you're a eugenicist or one of those rigid, furious yuppies who insist on being called "child-free." "Sure, the country was full of trees," said my friend Doug, a left-wing economics journalist. "Trees and *racists*." He was holding his newborn baby at the time, so perhaps I had chosen the wrong moment to bring up the subject of population growth. But isn't it strange that nobody talks about it anymore? On the right, it conflicts with anti-abortion big-Christian-family values—besides, talking about overpopulation might suggest that global warming is not a hoax perpetrated by Al Gore. On the Left, you're supposed to blame not population per se, sheer exponentially proliferating numbers, but our wasteful habits and lack of proper land-use laws, our cars, our fast food, our disposable shopping malls and edge cities and office parks. But what if that is just the way Americans are, so the more of us there are, the more we are like that? Maybe we needed that forest around us, like Bengal tigers, to cushion our rapacity. After all, even if we started to reverse course right now, we couldn't undo the damage we've already inflicted. Our spread-out suburbs are not going to contract into the compact villages of children's books with a main street full of little shops and countryside all around. The Hammocks may turn out to be an eyesore or it may be inoffensive or even pleasant, but most of all, it will be permanent—as permanent as anything gets in the twenty-first century. That long green view is never coming back.

I know what you're thinking: I must be depressed or disappointed or just a curmudgeon, a crab, one of those middle-aged purists who stopped listening to music when the

Beatles broke up. And it's true that I still miss the old Penn Station and the lower Manhattan waterfront when it was run-down and silent, with grass growing through cracks in the sidewalk—almost the same street Melville might have seen if he took a walk down from the customshouse at lunch, not a historical theme park where college kids buy pornwear at Abercrombie and brokers get drunk after work. And yes, I do think there is something embarrassing about middle-aged white women who claim to love gangsta rap for the energy and confess to maternal feelings for Eminem. In fact, even the thought of rap makes my heart surge with sorrow and fury because it is connected with other thoughts that are even more disturbing—about the end of melody, the end of tender and delicate feelings, the end of any sort of verbal cleverness that requires a vocabulary of more than three hundred words, the end of two hundred years of black genius that brought us blues and jazz and gospel and Motown despite everything we did to them. Where, as R. Crumb put it so well, is the beautiful music of our grandparents? Perhaps that is the problem right there.

These are things you're not supposed to say. Unless you are a famous, elegant, brilliant black person you're not supposed to go around saying you hate 50 Cent and don't even believe that he was shot nine times. You're not supposed to go on about badgers and glaciers and horrible new buildings. Young people can do that—anxiety and agitation and urgency are charming in the young, especially if they are beautiful, like Julia Butterfly up in that redwood. Even the despair of the young is appealing in a way, because it lets their elders feel wise and superior—if only they could see how time passes and things come right in the end! If they'd managed to get through just that one terrible week, maybe even just one really bad day, Werther could have gotten over Charlotte and enrolled in medical school like a sensible young German and Sylvia Plath, still trim and handsome in her seventies, could be drinking martinis with her fifth husband at their weekend place in Columbia County. "Remember when we were all so terrified of nuclear war?" he'd ask, stirring up the fire with a hand-forged poker they'd found at a barn auction, and she'd flash him her famous smile and say, "Funny how things work out." She hardly ever thinks about Ted, although when he died she wept and was surprised.

Still, I wasn't always like this. For a long time I thought things were getting better—uglier, yes, but more just and equal. I thought that little by little people were becoming less cruel, less stupid, less ignorant, less unfair. And they are, too—think of how much less racist white people are, how far women have come. And what about gay marriage? Ten years ago nobody'd even heard of it and now half the country has already moved on to gay divorce. And yet, you don't hear people looking forward to the future in the rapturous way they did back when they believed in some big triumphant idea like science or reason or socialism or art, or even a small, cozy hope like everyone having a place to live and nobody having to eat cat food. People might be excited about their own personal future—I still feel that sometimes; I get a little thrill just wondering which tulips will come back next spring. But when they think about the future in general, they're scared. Even the mad Christians don't seem to look forward to it, being whisked off to Heaven just like that. It's more like something they use to make other people jealous: God likes me best!

It's not as if I like being like this. People who despair after a certain age are just depressing. We don't have the looks for it, and besides, we make others uncomfortable: what if we're on to something? Sure, we're boring, always rambling on about how much better everything was back in our childhoods, when there was snow, but we might just be right. Nobody wants to believe that. Once you get over your youthful intensities you're supposed to look on the bright side, like parents. You're supposed to say, *There, there*. Nobody wants a mother who looks at Long Island Sound and starts talking about floating Bangladeshis; it's like having a mother who asks why you don't put dead people in your finger paintings. Up until recently, I did well in the role of maternal optimist. When my daughter would say, "It's quite a world you people are leaving us," I would joke and say, "Yes, and it started out so well" or, more briskly, "Just finish the bits around the edges and everything will be fine." And then I would give a brief inspirational speech about the power of human ingenuity to solve the most intractable problems. You people. The grown-ups. Me.

I actually believe it about human ingenuity. People can think themselves out of anything, and they like to do it, too; it's a challenge, like Sudoku or sculpting swans out of butter. There are so many great ideas out there: cars that run on used French-fry oil, and braziers for deforested places that use hardly any charcoal, and radios that wind up like Victrolas and never need new batteries. There would be bigger ideas, too, if enough people were paid to dream them up and put them into practice. That's why it's so strange that at exactly the pivotal moment, the last little window of time, we've gone so passive. It's not for lack of information, either. Al Gore is all over the place, and the news is full of bulletins. The glaciers of Greenland are melting twice as fast as previously believed. An island off the Indian coast has disappeared beneath the sea. Polar bears are starving because the ice is too weak for them to get out on it to hunt seals. Polar bears! Not some obscure insect or a fish with an ugly name like "mudbelly" or "swampsucker," but famous furry mammals beloved by children. We should be storming Congress and lying down in traffic, but we're not. We're not doing much of anything beyond signing Internet petitions and eating tilapia, which is supposed to be ecological but most of the time is actually some other, nonecological fish in disguise. Every now and then some anarchist boy sets fire to a couple of SUVs and gets put in jail for a long time. And once in a while a trickster comes along with something that sounds like fun, like those bumper stickers that read "I'm Changing the Climate! Ask Me How," and he gets a ton of publicity because we'd so, so love to believe there was some small, clever thing we could do that would make a difference, especially if it involved the behavior of someone other than ourselves. The idea was to plaster the sticker, guerrilla-style, on unattended SUVs. I actually bought some, but whenever I thought about creeping out at three in the morning to paste them on a Ford Explorer, I pictured the enraged, enormous owner leaping up out of nowhere and bashing my head in with a tire iron. Defacing cars is the sort of thing you probably don't want to do by yourself.

Maybe we've lost so much already, that we can't relate to what's left: the one building that's preserved when the rest of the street is torn down, the dusty bits of nature we fence off and visit on weekends, pretending we can't see the highway through the trees. In Rome I saw a baroque fountain marooned on a traffic island. It wasn't one of the famous ones, but it was still sad to see that lovely heap of sinuous mythological-allegorical marble sitting all by itself in a boiling tangle of cars. Maybe we need not just the rare, special things but what lay around them. Once that's gone the special things look forlorn and out of place, like Bengal tigers in the zoo or people who've lived too long. It's like when T. S. Eliot died and Ezra Pound, who hadn't seen him in years, said, so plaintively, "Who is there now for me to share a joke with?" That's old age: you look around, and the room is full of strangers. Death starts looking homelike; it's where your friends are.

Saul Bellow speaks somewhere about being in "departure mode": you stop caring, because you're getting ready to leave. When my grandmother turned seventy she gave away her nice things—her old silver teapot, her brass trays from India—because she'd decided to live simply, like a Buddhist. We thought she was getting ready to die—maybe she intuited some physical problem that a doctor had yet to find? But she lived another twenty years, drinking stewed tea from the old brown pot and watching Georgetown fancify itself beyond all recognition. When they tore down the Woolworth's on M Street it was as if they'd bulldozed the last real place, the last place that just was what it was, where you could pick up a spool of thread and some Alberto VO5 shampoo and sit at the counter with a sandwich, watching the world go by.

It wasn't that she wanted to die, not at all—but little by little, as the world became less familiar, less itself, she detached. Perhaps that's happening to me, too; I read an article about, say, movie stars and I realize, first of all, that they all look alike, even the ones I've seen in a film, and, second, that I don't care. It doesn't seem important to be able to tell them apart. I don't want to see their sex videos, either. So perhaps that is the beginning of departure mode, like listening only to the music you liked before you were thirty-five, and having a general sense of things vanishing but not being able to recall exactly what they were, just that taken all together they gave the world beauty and coherence and sense. Perhaps one of these days I'll feel myself drifting off into the sky, like a balloon.

The truth is, by the time you find out what's happening, it's usually too late. They've gotten the permits and filed their plans and pacified whoever they needed to, while you're still wondering, What's the story on those yellow markers in the field across from the cemetery? and thinking, I should ask Cindy about them. There was never a moment when the people in town who cared could have stopped the

Hammocks. It's like the turquoise frogs—by the time scientists figured out what was wrong with them, they were gone. I drive the other way and spend more time on the Internet. There, you make your own world. If you don't want to see something, you click and it disappears.

~

The other night I went to a party in the Village for a friend who'd just published a novel—a very good one that was getting fantastic reviews. One critic even called it great. It should have been a joyful occasion—she'd been struggling her whole life, and now critical glory! Nonetheless, the party was tinged with gloom. The agents and editors sailed briskly about in expensive colorful clothes, but the novelists and short-story writers leaned against walls with glasses of wine and and alternated between congratulating the guest of honor and commiserating with each other over the decline of the audience for fiction—even calling readers "the audience" tells you there's a problem—although maybe they were just hungry, since there was nothing to eat beyond a few dishes of nuts and a single small bowl of cherry tomatoes. People are reading less, we all know that. Soon writers will be consoling themselves that at least they're not classical musicians. Those people are *really* screwed.

What people mostly wanted to talk about, though, was the apartment itself. The place was like a warm brown cave, narrow and twisty and softly lit, with furniture that looked as if it had been rescued from the street and patiently refinished by hand. The host, who had written three books of increasing convolution and darkness—the reviewers' comparisons progressed from Austen to Proust to Kafka—had covered every wall with paintings. The word was that he had bought them all on eBay for next to nothing. Most were small portraits in oils—serious children, women with hair pulled back and strong plain faces, young men in baggy suits who looked like they could use a good meal. It was obvious that they were old pictures; people don't look like that anymore, self-contained and somehow formal even in ordinary clothes. The general effect of seeing so many of them together was of a shrine to memory—other people's memory. The picture that drew my eye, though, was a big landscape of flat, watery fields and a row of dark trees lit by golden light. It was from Denmark, the host told me, and like all his other art, much of which was also Danish, he had found it in eBay's Modern Painting section, which went from 1900 through 1949. That seemed like a funny definition of modern—I'd always thought I lived in the modern era, but apparently it ended the year I was born.

Since then, I've been looking in on eBay. It's not that I want to start collecting—even if I had the wall space and the disposable cash, I don't have the patience to click through page after page of mostly terrible pictures— impressionist copies, Vermont snow scenes, imitation Georgia O'Keeffes—and hover over the auctions of the rare good ones, waiting to zap the competition at the last minute. But there's something compelling too about that jumble of painted lumber; it's like a giant garage sale of history, with justusintexas and mamabear425 fighting for the privilege of paying over a thousand dollars for a painting of lilacs that may be "late Victorian" but is almost certainly not by the once well-known artist and president of the National Academy of Design J. Alden Weir. I like to wander around the Modern Paintings, Realist section just to look at those old-fashioned faces, those forest pathways and spring bouquets in a jar. Besides, I tell myself, there may be a picture buried in there of the view from Beach Park Road—there were quite a few minor painters in this part of Connecticut at one time; it's quite likely that pictures of those very fields exist. Or, if not of that exact view, there may be a picture of another view very much like it, perhaps in Denmark. Most of the paintings I like seem to come from there. There are certain similarities: the flatness, the many greens, the sea off in the distance, the thin marine blue of the sky.

MRS. RAZZMATAZZ

MY MOTHER DIED IN 1979, BUT I DIDN'T SEE HER FBI file until four years later. My father requested it when he asked the Bureau for his own. "What's this all about?" I asked him on the phone. "It says here that in November and December 1960 Mama was 'under the care of a physician for complications of pregnancy.'" I would have just turned eleven—could she have been ill for two months and I not remember? "Oh, that—that was nothing," he said, but it was obvious he was lying. "What do you mean, nothing?" I said. "There must have been something to it; I'm reading it right here from the page." The FBI might have framed the Rosenbergs, but I knew they weren't making *this* up, whatever it was. Finally he said in a rush, "Oh, all right! All right! You really want to know? Your mother had an abortion and she didn't tell me." Well, whose fault was that, I didn't say. "When I found out afterwards, I was angry." I'll bet, I didn't say. Then he said, "I wonder which of her women friends was the informer."

I didn't blame my mother for not telling my father. Hadn't I had a pregnancy scare and said nothing about it to the man I was then living with till it was over? I should have kept even more secrets from men than I did. My mother probably knew my father would have tried to change her mind. "It's not just tissue in there," he often said in later years when he and I argued about abortion. Besides, he loved children—he was always inviting kids from down the block over to meet the cat or see what was new in the garden. I'll bet he would have fought hard to keep her from getting rid of this one if he had known it was *in there*. He told me once that when their young single friend Maxine had gotten pregnant, back in the 1950s, he had offered to adopt the baby. My mother was the one who gave Maxine the five hundred dollars for the operation—an enormous sum in those days. Mostly I felt sorry for my mother having to go through an illegal abortion—the secrecy and fear, the pain and blood, those "complications of pregnancy" the FBI was so interested in. And alone, too. That was the worst part. Not that she went behind my father's back, but that she felt she needed to.

People talk about feminists as being anti-motherhood, but I never would have had my daughter if it hadn't been for the women's movement. From what I saw growing up, becoming a mother was the end of being yourself—you might as well have a lobotomy and get it over with. I didn't know anyone like the mothers in the Mrs. Piggle-Wiggle books I loved, women who sewed Halloween costumes and baked from scratch, and who seemed perfectly happy taking care of their big old houses, funny children, and ever-so-slightly dim-witted husbands. Our little street in Brooklyn was full of women who seethed with bottled-up energy and got just a little bit weirder with each passing year. Patsy's mom, chainsmoking in her doorway, watching the comings and goings of her neighbors with her witchy black eyes, was weird—you had to pretend to be in a big hurry when you walked by or she'd try to involve you in some long, urgent, off-key conversation—and so was Janet's mom, pacing her beautiful brownstone like a panther, turning out the occasional wild, huge oil painting in between the children, the husband, the three meals a day. Annie's mom wasn't weird, she just drank a lot. But then there was no Annie's dad to explain that the reason Annie's mom got mad for no reason was that she was about to get her period.

It was feminism that let me see a woman could have children—well, one or two—and still have her life, maybe even a richer, intenser life because a child was another person to love. And it was feminism that made it an expected, an ordinary, thing for a man and a woman to live together in their own way—they could clean the house together or just let it fall apart. Those were not ideas that you could easily derive from middle-class American family life in the 1950s and 1960s, even a family of Communists like mine. Who owned the means of production—that was nothing, that could change overnight. But who vacuumed, who brought coffee while the other person remained seated, who held forth and who made encouraging murmurs—that seemed set in stone. I had to see lots of people my age living together and getting married and still making dinner together, and have it sink into my stubborn brain that most of my close friends who became mothers might take a bit of time off but basically kept on with work they cared about, and I had to read endless articles about women writers having babies and continuing to publish book after book, sometimes even books that said new and shocking things about being a mother, before I could imagine that life for myself. If it hadn't been for feminism I would have been a very different person. I might have lost myself entirely in a man, or men—I could have worked up quite a line in romantic slavery masquerading as rebellion against convention. Or I might have gone totally the other way and become a solitary, living in books and words, making poems out of decades-old infatuations and the changing blue of the sky.

~

My mother was smart, beautiful, idealistic and kind, her father's adored *shayna madel*, the star of New Utrecht High. She could play the Moonlight sonata so movingly that Mrs. Greenberg next door stopped slicing potatoes to listen, she could recite Heine's poems in German, she could tell you what President Roosevelt was up to any hour of the day or night, and Mrs. Roosevelt too. She was radical even then. What kind of God, she asked the rabbi, would kill the first-born sons of the Egyptians? What had those little boys ever done to Him? I have the ring she designed for herself at sixteen—a blue zircon blossoming through gold prison bars. At the University of Wisconsin and afterward, she picketed segregated restaurants, she marched in demonstrations; when her beloved Walter Gieseking played Carnegie Hall, she sided with the protesters, because face it, darling, he might be a great pianist but he was a Nazi collaborator too. I sometimes wondered if I had half-imagined the scene of the two big men looming in the hall and her shutting the door in their faces—did FBI agents really wear hats and trench coats like the lawmen in *Dragnet* and *I Led Three Lives*? Maybe not, but the incident itself is noted in her file as having happened on May 4, 1955. ("POLLITT, while exhibiting a cordial manner advised the agents that she did not desire to be interviewed by agents of the FBI, relative to matters concerning the Communist Party.") I could hear the tension in her voice, and sense the fear that made her stand up extra straight, but she shooed those agents away as if they were door-to-door salesmen intruding on her busy day. "I don't have to talk to you," she said, "and I'm not going to." In fact, if they had been salesmen, she probably would have bought something. She would have felt sorry for them, having to work so hard and smile all the time.

My mother had her dream self, like we all do. She told me that she was named Leanora, after the heroine of *Fidelio*, the brave girl who rescues her lover from prison. Actually, her name was plain Lenore, after her grandmother Lonnie, who had borne eight children back in

Russia, and died of a septic abortion just before the First World War. Her dream self would be a journalist like Dorothy Thompson, or maybe a fiery revolutionary like La Pasionaria, or both; she would give lots of parties and have closets full of elegant clothes and go to the theater and the ballet and the opera whenever she wanted. And at first the dream seemed to be moving right along: college at sixteen, Columbia Law at twenty, nine proposals before she met my father, she told me proudly, and you could see why—she must have been irresistible, with those big dark eyes in that delicate little face, with her cashmere sweaters, her delicious cloud of Chanel No 5. It was terribly romantic and exciting, how she fell for my father, her law-school classmate, the first time she saw him, on a picket line—"He looked like Leslie Howard, so tall and handsome, with the sun in his hair"— and three months later eloped with him to Newburgh, because his mother didn't want her son marrying a Jew. Five days later, my mother dropped out of law school.

Was that the point at which she began to lose herself? It's hard for me to imagine her as a practicing lawyer—she was too dreamy, too unaggressive, too nice—but if she had gotten her degree she would have set a precedent for herself, of achieving something both difficult and validated by the world. That might have helped her figure out a way to be the writer she imagined becoming. She told me she applied to Columbia on a whim, and that she hated law school. But she also told me she had probably been accepted only because it was easy for women to get in—the men were still off in the army. Yet the 1946 yearbook shows only a few female faces in a sea of men. Among that handful of eager, brightly smiling future women lawyers my mother looks pensive and shy.

If you try to explain people's behavior by their circumstances—poor people who mug and steal and deal drugs, abused children who grow up and beat their own kids—someone is sure to accuse you of excusing them. After all, lots of people endure the same conditions and don't turn out that way. Newspapers love stories of miraculous survival—the homeless teenager who gets herself to college on a full scholarship, the drug addict who pulls himself back from the brink of death and becomes a counselor to others.

Stories like that let us believe in free will, despite all the evidence against it. Free will, after all, implies choice, which implies knowledge, and how much knowledge—usable knowledge, not the kind sitting on the shelf—do people really have in the thick of life? Was there an actual moment when my mother said, Today is the day I am failing to claim myself, or If I keep drinking I am choosing to become an alcoholic, or This is the bottle of vodka that will give me cirrhosis, so do I pour it down the sink or not? It wasn't like Adam and Eve with the apple, or Macbeth with the phantom knife. Or maybe it was, maybe she felt the whole time that she was going down a terrible, shameful, dangerous path, and that was why she had to try very hard to keep her drinking secret.

And the amazing thing was, she did. Even after the doctor diagnosed the cirrhosis, we didn't know how she'd done it. I never saw my mother drink to get drunk, just a bourbon before dinner at home, a vodka martini or two in a restaurant. And yet she was drunk a great deal of the time for years—a condition my father called "being irrational," "being hostile," or "about to get/having/recently having had her period." "Why are we celebrating the deaths of those little Egyptian boys, anyway," she would say bitterly out of nowhere every year at our family seder. It was only after she died that the little pint bottles became visible to us, as if a spell had been broken. We must have found a dozen, carefully positioned sideways in the kitchen cabinets with the old aluminum pots, mingling with the Mr. Clean and Bab-O under the sink, standing quietly in the back of the coat closet, among the winter boots.

~

It is hard to imagine there was ever a time when the language of alcoholism treatment didn't permeate ordinary speech, but I was twenty-nine when the concept of denial was explained to me by Dr. Borecky, the only physician who, much too late, treated my mother for what she actually had; the others had been as reluctant to put a name to it as my father or I and preferred to talk about vitamin deficiencies and obscure brain conditions. Because of course we had known, in a way, all along. Other mothers didn't offer their daughters' friends old Halloween candy for breakfast after a sleepover. By high school I knew not to bring friends over after school, because my mother might be "behaving irrationally," dozing on the sofa, then waking with a wild, startled look. "What? What did you say?" she would ask in a strange, harsh voice, but nobody had been speaking. My parents, who had loved parties and get-togethers with friends, withdrew into their own world. At my college graduation she took small, tired steps like an old woman— at forty-six—and was hospitalized the following week with delirium tremens. Even that didn't open our eyes: when she was home again she insisted she was through with drinking, and it seemed wrong not to believe her. After all, we loved her: she was my mother, who had told me the story of *La Boheme* as if it was all about how poor Mimi was; she was my father's charming, beautiful wife, the girl he had run off with all those years ago. Now and then my father would have a flare-up of recognition. He would look into moving to a dry county in South Carolina, or try to find a doctor who would give my mother Antibuse, a drug that makes you sick if you drink, without telling her what it was. "I think your mother might be drinking again," he said once during those years. "I think she puts it in that spicy tomato juice she always keeps in the fridge. But I'm just not sure." "Why don't you drink it yourself," I said meanly, "and see if you get drunk?" We behaved just like the clueless, moralistic relatives in those addiction memoirs everyone makes fun of now. Unfortunately, those books had not been written yet. I probably could have learned a lot from them.

Dr. Borecky, the good doctor, made my father and me both go to Al-Anon. There, other people living with alcoholics told us to Detach with Love, but what kind of love was that? Weren't we here on earth to save each other? I never understood how detaching with love was different than smiling benignly while you watch someone drown. The great thing about Al-Anon for me wasn't the philosophy—those sunny catchphrases like "Easy does it" (Easy does what?), let alone the problematic issue of the Higher Power (who?). It was the people. I had friends whose parents were alcoholics, rather a lot of them, actually—is it just that there were so many, or did we seek each other out without knowing?—but we never talked about it frankly and straightforwardly and concretely, the way these strangers, ordinary people gathered in a church hall on their lunch hour or after work, did with each other. A white-haired man in a zip-up cardigan sweater told me to call anytime and gave me his card—he had a shop on Amsterdam Avenue that repaired and sold caned chairs. I kept that card in my bedside drawer for years, and although I never did call him, I knew if I did he would be glad to talk to me. It wouldn't matter whether or not he remembered me. I felt safe and protected just passing by his store and seeing the chairs hanging from the ceiling through the big second-floor window.

The Adult Children of Alcoholics meetings, which I wandered into thinking they were the same as Al-Anon, were pitched on more familiar psychological terrain: everything bad in your life is your parents' fault. Their bedrock principle was that alcoholics did not love their children; taking this in, understanding that their gestures of love were only for show, because obviously they preferred drinking to you, was part of the healing work, as was accepting that you yourself were damaged in predictable ways, of which there

was a list so vague and so long and so internally contra-
dictory (if people "have low self-esteem," can they also
"take themselves very seriously"?) that who on earth could
fail to find themselves there? Take "judge themselves without mercy." Even if that is a bad thing—was St. John of
the Cross an adult child of an alcoholic?—wouldn't it
undermine the validity of one's yes answers to the other
questions? Maybe you don't "constantly seek approval and
affirmation from others," you just think you do because
you're so hard on yourself. As for "thinking that you are different from other people," doesn't the list supposedly enu-
merate those differences? In fact, I couldn't see that the children of alcoholics were so different from the children of
nonalcoholics—"have difficulty with intimate relation-
ships" is practically a definition of being human, at least in
New York. But then, it was hard to find a control group.
Once you started paying attention, there were alcoholic
parents everywhere.

~

When I was a child I was a real daddy's girl—my mother
looked up to him, so why wouldn't I? He was the one who
said, It's a beautiful day, let's go ride the Staten Island Ferry;
let's walk across the Brooklyn Bridge; who, if I wondered
what a ballroom was, would ask the man at the St. George
Hotel if we could take a look at theirs. He was the one for
songs and jokes. "I shall be an old bum, / loved but unre-
spected," he sang as he shaved in the morning. "Look, it's
Mrs. Razzmatazz," he would say when we drove past Green-

Wood Cemetery at night and the beams of our headlights made a faint, pale flickering against the railings that seemed to be traveling alongside us. "Mrs. Razzmatazz, the ghost." As I got older, my allegiance shifted—now it embarrassed me that she asked the same naïve questions to elicit the same pontificating answers, that when we walked down the street she trailed two steps behind him, like a Muslim wife. If she couldn't keep up with his long strides, why didn't he slow down for her? In our family stories, my mother had the role of the impractical, sheltered one: "Help, there's a dead chicken in the icebox!" she had cried out as a newlywed, when my father's mother had stocked the refrigerator as a surprise. But by the time I was ten or eleven, my mother had started selling real estate—she could make her own hours and she was tired of worrying about money—and she turned out to be very good at it. The Brooklyn Heights brownstone revival was just getting under way, and from that moment on she earned a lot more than my father, which was quite a feat back then. But it was still back then: when my father had made more, my mother cleaned and tidied and cooked; when my mother made more, she cleaned and tidied and cooked. It didn't matter that she was a terrible cook, who broiled steaks to shoe leather and put wheat germ in the beef stroganoff to be "creative." Nor did it matter that my father worked at home, loved good food, and enjoyed his occasional forays into the kitchen. She was the wife; the wife made the meals, no matter how much money she earned. When we went to our favorite restaurant, Whyte's, the old fish place down on Fulton Street, my mother passed my father cash for the bill under the table. Who was that scenario enacted for? Mr. Phillips, the head waiter? Me? Each other? She might have been a successful businesswoman and a radical with her own FBI file, but she still subscribed to *McCall's* and the *Ladies' Home Journal* and *Good Housekeeping*, where the protection of the "fragile male ego" was the top item on the wifely to-do list.

It was around the time that my mother was slipping those tens and twenties under the table that she had that abortion the FBI so delicately mentioned. You can see how she had to do it. How she had to draw the line somewhere, and how she had to not let him know.

～

My mother had majored in journalism, and had even worked briefly at the *Daily News,* writing picture captions for the sports page. But the only published work I ever saw of hers was—maybe—the anonymous entry for Richard III in the Columbia Encyclopedia, where she had a temp job as a researcher. She told me she had tried to subtly inveigle into the dry language her sympathy for Richard, history's underdog, and sometimes when I read that entry over I can see a ghostly effect. "Some historians have maintained that Shakspere's interpretation of Richard is unjust but the impression remains." "Unjust" sounds so like her. Mostly she transferred her ambitions to me—I would be the writer. She sat at the kitchen table and listened to me read out loud my poems about Greek mythology and my long, boring imitations of *The Three Musketeers*. She clipped poems by

Cavafy from *Vogue* and mailed them to me at camp along with clippings from the *National Guardian* about all the great things Fidel was doing in Cuba. When I wanted to learn Ancient Greek, she found a Brooklyn College student to teach me. "Bad writing drives out good," she warned me when, like everyone else in tenth grade, I became obsessed with Mia Farrow and Ryan O'Neal in *Peyton Place*. I have often wondered whether that is true. Maybe great writing can drive out good writing, and my mother would have given herself more of a chance if she had idealized litera- ture less.

~

Dr. Borecky got my mother into Smithers, the rehab facil- ity housed in Billy Rose's vast old marble mansion on East Ninety-third St. Rehab: another word you didn't hear much back then. After two weeks she walked out. "I was home- sick," she told me on the phone, "and the other people were all drug addicts. I can beat this thing on my own." I said ter- rible things and hung up on her. She called me back a few minutes later, and that is why the last words I ever heard her say were "I love you." A few days later she was in a coma. "You had your mother longer than I had mine," said Aunt Goldie in the hospital waiting room. "When my mother died, I was only fourteen." By Aunt Goldie's old-country standards, I was lucky to have had my mother as long as I did. "We hoped she might pull through, she was so young," said the kind nurse. Only fifty-four. Younger than I am now.

The night before she died I slept on the couch in my parents' house to be near the hospital, the same beat-up Danish Modern one on which she used to doze and startle all those years ago. I dreamed we were all up in my grandparents' house on Lake Mahopac, my aunts and uncles, my cousins, my father, me; even the Weisses, the old Orthodox couple next door, were there. It was a beautiful summer afternoon, we were all sitting around the big picnic table, which was heaped with my grandmother's food: roast chicken, cantaloupe slices, cinnamon-raisin cake from her own mother's recipe—dead Lonnie's recipe that she carried across the ocean in her head. There was something strange and flickering about the light, though—it was as if I was watching an old home movie. At first my mother wasn't there, and then, somehow, she was sitting right next to me. "You're here," I said to her, my heart flooded with relief. "How did you get here?" "They said I have to go back," she said slyly, as if she had gotten away with something. "But not just yet."

~

I know a lot of women—feminists, too—who have bad feelings about their mothers: anger, resentment, disapproval. They might be fifty, but they sound like they're fifteen. Moreover, they assume all women feel this way. Once I suggested at a gathering that a writer in our circle could have been a little more sympathetic to her mother in her memoir about her father's Alzheimer's—after caring for her always difficult and now demented husband for many, many years, the mother, by then in her seventies, took up with a widower she met at a self-help group. Everyone looked at me as if I'd suggested we all become born-again Christians. I decided this wasn't the moment to wonder out loud how come women blame their mothers for all their faults and problems but take for themselves all the credit for their virtues and accomplishments. Later, a friend suggested that the women who resent their mothers are the ones whose mothers were strong-willed, efficient, domestically competent and proud of it—you know, like mothers are supposed to be. They made their daughters feel they couldn't measure up. My mother wasn't like that. She never nudged me about getting married or criticized my hair or clothes or suggested I choose a career that combined well with children. She wanted me to feel that I could do anything. Except, of course, keep her from drinking.

Sometimes in those years when my mother was being "irrational," when I was sitting reading or doing my homework, she would touch my hair as she passed by. I hated that gesture; it seemed so humble, so tentative, so fearful. For God's sake stand up for yourself, I would think—Don't let him be the stronger. Don't let *me* be the stronger. I'd have to fight the urge to growl and swat her hand away. It wasn't till years after her death that I saw that touching me like that was her way of reassuring herself: I was there, I was all right, I was her precious growing daughter, safe and happy with my book. It was a protective gesture, and what she was protecting me from was herself.

I think now and then about that brother or sister I didn't have, that forty-six-year-old person who could be anyone to me by now, my dearest confidante or a voice making a duty phone call once a year from California. But to tell you the truth, I don't grieve that he or she's not here. Let the unborn bury the unborn. My mother's is the unlived life that I mourn. The Al-Anon people would say I never learned to Detach with Love, and that is true. I still believe we let her slip away——my father, me, those stupid doctors with their vitamins. "Your mother just ran out of time," one therapist said. And I've read that the typical alcoholic falls off the wagon nine times before she gives up drinking for good. If she ever does. Still, I know that when I cry for her there's guilt mixed in with the grief. My father felt the same: "I'm sorry I didn't save your mother," he told me before the attendants wheeled him away for a quadruple bypass, at eighty-three. Not couldn't, didn't.

~

One night shortly after my mother died, I took a taxi home because it was raining. Somewhere along Ninth Avenue I glimpsed a little coffee shop with a neon sign out front: a yellow sun and a bright blue palm tree. It was like a child's drawing, lighting up the dark, wide street. I thought about all the little pleasures and experiences my mother had forgone, and now would never have, because she had spent so much of her life drinking—like taking a walk and stopping in for a cup of coffee someplace just because there was a blue palm tree shining over the door. At that moment, and for a long time afterward, it seemed to me that her life had been entirely wasted, and I was furious at her.

It was only when I had my own child that I could begin to see her life differently. Watching Sophie become her own self, I thought that whatever anger and disappointments my mother felt about her life—and she must have been angry, that was what came out when she drank—she must have had a lot of the same pleasures I was having now. It's a blurry line between parents and children, so maybe she hadn't minded as much as I once believed that she hadn't become a writer. Maybe that had always been more a fantasy than a real ambition, and maybe it was enough for her that I was living it out.

I decided to believe that she had made it her life task not to pass on her damage to me, to give me good gifts, including ones she had been unable to give herself. And, not right away, but eventually, I decided to believe that she succeeded.

I LET MYSELF GO

One

AT THE END OF MY FORTIES, I LET MYSELF GO. I gained twenty pounds—oh, all right, twenty-five. I let my hair go seriously two-tone between colorings and I stopped wearing what little makeup I had used before. True, in a moment of panic I joined a gym, but I only went four times. Each swim and sauna ended up costing two hundred dollars. Sometimes I thought of that wasted money with shame: if I wasn't going to exercise, why not admit it and send an African girl—twelve African girls—to high school? Other times I thought it served some sort of psychological purpose, as a kind of burnt offering on the altar of Musculus, god of fitness: *Please don't let me have a heart attack, I'm trying to figure this out!* From time to time I would look in the mirror and be horrified at the pale pink seal-woman floundering there, but most of the time I tried not to think about it. After all, the man I lived with told me every day that he loved me, even if he also said, when pressed, that he didn't mind that I was fat.

There was a precedent here. My mother stayed thin as a girl her whole life, but she gave up on her looks about the same time I did. As a young woman she had been a dark-eyed beauty who enjoyed being told she looked like Jackie Kennedy and who loved to wear elegant things from Bonwit Teller and Martin's and other stores that no longer exist. When she reached her mid-forties, she stopped bothering with all that. She moved into jeans and T-shirts and Keds, let her hair go gray, and quit having it styled. She simply parted it on one side and pinned it with a plastic barrette, like a child. She quit wearing makeup too. The old-fashioned cake of dark-brown mascara with its stiff little brush, with which I taught myself how to put on eye make-up before leaving for college, was still in the bathroom cabinet when she died a decade later.

~

When I was married I didn't pay much attention to my looks, and when I got divorced I paid even less. I wore my favorite gray T-shirt until you could see through it, like a spider web. You might say I trusted in my powers of conversation to charm and beguile, like a man, or you might say I had abandoned the field completely rather than engage in a degrading beauty contest that I felt sure to lose. I would picture T. S. Eliot living like a monk in that rectory, forty-five going on sixty, and it seemed like a sensible choice, to give up intentionally what you are going to be forced to relinquish anyway and to move on to the next stage, some Zennish way of being, but with meat. And yet, I would rage at the way American women are sidelined sexually as they get older. T. S. Eliot got a second wind and married his secretary. Why couldn't America be like France, where older women are seen as attractive, like Charlotte Rampling in *Under the Sand?* Maybe the difference isn't the men but the women, my boyfriend said dryly. Maybe Frenchwomen make more of an effort. Yes, I thought bitterly, they probably do. The slaves.

～

Everything had become too symbolic for me; perhaps that was the problem. Dressing fashionably, wearing makeup, dieting—obviously, these were conformist measures, acquiescence in sex-objectification. What is more pathetic than a man and woman at a restaurant, he digging into a hearty steak with fries while she fiddles with an exotic salad and sips a Perrier decorated with a delicate fan of lime? She's worse than a pale young lady of the nineteenth century displaying ethereality by refusing refreshments at a ball; that young lady probably ate a hearty nineteenth-century dinner at home first. How can Steak Man not feel that Lettuce Woman is denying herself to please him and wants him to see her doing so? I wished I could see these feminine activities as just part of the play of life, sex, pleasure—only what could be pleasurable about living on salad and water? The pleasure was not in the experience itself but in its intended effect on others—on incarnating an image, one that curiously combined self-denial and pleasure, weakness and strength, having less self and having more self. On the other hand, who wanted to be old and fat? Women who argued that losing your looks was no loss were like deaf-rights activists who claimed they weren't missing anything by not being able to hear.

You could wander among these contradictions for years, and that is what I did.

Two

MY FRIEND JON SAYS YOU CAN ALWAYS TELL A face-lift. Not at first, perhaps, if the doctor is really skillful, but after a few years the lower half of the face separates from the top; a line develops across the top of the cheekbones, like the pure sharp line between the custard and the fluff in a lemon meringue pie. Living in Los Angeles, Jon gets a lot of practice. "Look," he'll say, pointing to some gaunt, bejeweled producer's wife in the audience when we're watching an awards ceremony on TV. "See the line under the eye cavity? It's so obvious." There are other giveaways. Neck wrinkles: the face sits on top of them like a lustrous cellophaned lollipop on a grubby paper stick. Hands, with liver spots and ropy veins: they haven't figured out how to do hand-lifts yet.

It seems Jon should be right, but is he? After all, he never gets to verify his theory. You can't actually go up to people and ask if they've had cosmetic surgery. Perhaps the only face-lifts Jon detects are the cheap ones, the botched ones, the trout lips and visible scars like the ones posted on awfulplasticsurgery.com. Maybe those are the decoys, the ones you're supposed to notice. Perhaps all around us are more extremely clever plastic people than we know.

~

Ten years ago, twenty years ago, when popular feminism still clung to ideas like nature, comfort, "accepting your body," and every woman being beautiful "in her own way," I started hearing about feminists who had had cosmetic surgery. Gloria Steinem, according to one rumor, had her eyelids lifted—well, who could blame her, the poor woman could hardly see out from under them! Still, it put a spin on her famous "This is what fifty looks like." Sure, this is what fifty looks like—if you never eat a square meal and a surgeon remodels your face. A tall, athletic writer I knew slightly, very fiery and to me quite beautiful, got breast implants. She was in her late forties and thought it would help her get a boyfriend. I heard that she found one, too. Which was the exciting thing for him, I wonder, the plastic breasts or the scar on the underside? The pleasure or the knowledge of the suffering that produced it? Maybe both. "You want to know what silicone feels like?" asks Gwyn, the rich, self-satisfied, morally fraudulent hack novelist in Martin Amis's *The Information*. "It feels good. It feels better. Because of what it says." Implants say you're a go-getter, you've made your body into a product, a brand, the way Gwyn has made himself into a literary brand. The scar says you are willing to suffer in order to incarnate a collective fantasy, and also that you've made that fantasy so intimately your own that most of the time you can persuade yourself that it was all your own idea in the first place. Your choice.

That old-style feminism could be a real joy killer. Once you say the personal is political, which it is, it's hard to find a stopping place on the slippery slope that ends in Birkenstocks and vegan lo mein. But at least it offered a perspective from which to analyze and challenge some of the heavier social pressures on women. These days, feminism's motto is "You go, girl!" Anything is feminist as long as you "choose" it. In fact, it's unsisterly, patronizing, infantilizing, and sexist to question another woman's decision on any subject, no matter how dangerous or silly or servile or self-destructive it is; she is the captain of her soul and that's all you need to know. There's no social context and no place to stand and resist; there's just a menu of individual options and preferences. One writer I knew wrote about her face-lift in *Ms.* She was fifty-two, single, and wanted to stay in the sexual whirl for a few more years. True, no man in her left-literary-bohemian circle would contemplate having surgery to get a date, but what was she supposed to do with that fact? I ran into her a few months after the article came out. She looked great, zipping around Manhattan on her bicycle: toned, spandexed, her pale, oval face as smooth as a piece of paper under a spiky, dyed-black hairdo. Recently I saw her again: her hair was as black as ever, and her face was still unwrinkled, but now she looked oddly stiff and inexpressive, as if she was thinking about something else as she spoke. Her smile didn't reach her eyes. Botox? "She looks fantastic!" protested a mutual friend, another feminist. Who, come to think of it, seemed, since I last saw her, to have acquired the tipped eyes and upwardly slanted cheekbones of a cat.

Three

WALKING UP AND DOWN BROADWAY, IN AND OUT of stores on a Saturday afternoon, you see humanity in all its variety—old people with walkers, Caribbean women in pretty flowered dresses made in Malaysia and sold on the street by African men for ten dollars, harried parents herding their children from store to store, Orthodox Jewish couples, the women trim and vivacious, beautifully dressed for the Sabbath with their fancy wide-brimmed hats drawn down over their foreheads like 1940s movie stars, the men looking as if they'd just emerged from a basement, flabby and pale, in ill-fitting suits. I've lived in my neighborhood for a long time, and there are people I've seen on the street for fifteen years to whom I've assigned identities: the Businessman in a Hurry, the Anxious Screenwriter, Dostoyevsky—this last a filthy bearded barefoot man with the long greasy hair of a Russian monk, who panhandles on his knees with an agonized grimace and his arms thrown up as if in desperate prayer. I've watched the Businessman's mustache go white over the years and his figure go from trim to portly; the Screenwriter's put on weight too, but he still has pushy basketball player shoulders and he still projects an aura of hustle and frustration and worn sixties hipness: the ripped purple T-shirt, the unruly curls. I wonder if they have a name for me, and if they've noted the ways I look older too.

There is something both horrible and exciting about this human parade. It's like a scene from the nineteenth century—unsanitized, fleshy, saggy, gnarled, with the sweaty, fermented scent of rye bread. People have warts and big noses and hair sprouting from strange places: old men with eyebrows taking off like wings, old women with mustaches and thin hair barely covering a pinkly shining scalp. For years there was even a hunchback, a tiny ancient man with dead-white skin who wore a shabby black suit and walked bent at the waist as if looking for a dropped coin, oblivious to the people around him. It was as if he existed in a parallel dimension—1930s Warsaw, Kafka's Prague—and we could see him only because of a momentary quirk in the space-time continuum. It seems impossible that the radiant children capering ahead in their colorful Hanna Anderson outfits should ever turn into such as these.

Not everyone looks so individualized, though, now that the neighborhood's gone upscale. At fashionable restaurants, the ones with challenging menu items like pistachio-crusted Dover sole with grapefruit coulis and wine that costs double your phone bill, notice how many diners look like publicity photos—polished, soft-focused yet alert, leaning in to display their best features, their expression communicating some purposeful, simple idea like "manly lawyer" or "upbeat stay-at-home mom who exercises a lot." It's a kind of self-branding, a smoothing out not just of wrinkles and pouches but of the whole presentation. Are they concealing the parts of themselves that don't fit the public persona? Or, perhaps with the help of pharmaceuticals, have they truly discarded them, like the van Gogh posters and Indian bedspreads of their first apartment? Psychiatrists would say you can't escape yourself, that it all comes back to bite you in the end, but that's what psychiatrists would say, isn't it? Maybe they only see the bitten ones. The ones that mind being bitten, that is.

Four

I WAS ASTONISHED WHEN MY FRIEND DIANE TOLD me she'd had a nose job when she turned sixteen—her mother signed her up for it the way mothers used to sign their kids up to have their tonsils removed. If you had a "Jewish" nose, it was just what you did, like having an all-pink luncheon with your girlfriends for your sweet sixteen.

Now beautiful, birdlike, fifty but looking forty, Diane kneads and stretches her neck like pizza dough. "I don't want a face-lift, just to get rid of these sags under my chin." There are, in fact, no sags under her chin, just a charming roundedness, as in a picture of a pretty girl by Fragonard or Watteau. Her husband sighs and rolls his eyes. You can tell they've had this conversation many times. "No, I'm serious—for my next birthday I'm having a consultation." "My chin is much worse than yours," I say consolingly, as if that mattered.

~

If you could take a pill and wake up looking twenty years—or ten years, or six months—younger, who wouldn't? What joy to have the sags and bags of time all magically erased! After all, by the standards of most of human history, from forty on we're living like much younger people—falling in love, changing careers, climbing mountains. A century ago, most of us would be sick or widowed or dead, not signing up for intermediate French or Match.com. I don't have a single close friend my age with grandchildren; by their mid-fifties, my mother's mother had three and my father's mother had six. So why not look young too? I asked my friends how old they feel: eighteen said fifty-two-year-old Diane; late forties or early fifties said Alan, who is sixty-one. Katherine, fifty-eight, said she's decided to be fifty-one forever. I said thirty-seven, the year I had my daughter. Is there a refusal of wisdom and experience here—as if motherhood, that long, absorbing, hectic life, had left no mark and when my daughter leaves for college I can just pick up where I was before? Nobody said they felt their chronological age, let alone older.

But then, there are no good words to describe our time of life as it actually feels. "Older" raises the question of "older than whom?" "Midlife" is the upbeat new euphemism—there you are, in the thick of it!—but a fifty-five-year-old person is in the middle of his life only if he's going to live to 110. "Middle-aged" sounds tired and plodding, almost as bad as "aging"—and "aging" is sad and pitiful, an insult even though it's actually universally applicable. A fifty-year-old is aging at the same rate as a baby or a tree or a bottle of wine, exactly one second per second.

" 'Matronly' is a good word," says my friend Phyllis, who

is sixty, gently graying and as delicately boned as a gazelle. "It sounds powerful and serious and deserving of respect. I'd like to be a matron." The matrons of ancient Rome were famously powerful and respected, even feared, which must have been amusing for them, but do such women still exist? Maybe you can still find matrons in Europe. On upper Broadway you can always tell the older European women, with their below-the-knee skirts and dark cardigans and sensible low-heeled pumps, the way they carry themselves with a sense of decorum even when they are just doing the grocery shopping. We don't have American matrons now, though, and when we did, they were stuffy and conservative and ridiculous, like Margaret Dumont in the Marx Brothers movies or the book-clubbing women in Helen Hokinson's *New Yorker* cartoons. They had monobosoms and strict ideas about thank-you notes and chrysanthemums. There was nothing sexy about being a matron. It's depressing even to think of their underwear, the huge panties and boxy bras, maybe one of those Band-Aid-colored corsets one sometimes sees in the windows of medical supply stores. "Patron" suggests wealth, benevolence, and power, but today "matron" connotes a limited, grim, delegated authority, over children, prisoners, the sick. In Britain, a matron is a head nurse or a housemother in a boarding school. A matron who gives lots of money to museums or the opera gets a partial sex change: she becomes a patroness. Still, the dignity of a matron may be fragile, but at least she's got some. How much dignity does a fifty-five-year-old woman have who's starved and liposuctioned herself into a bikini meant for a teenager? Or a fifty-five-year-old man in a Speedo, for that matter? Are they the captains of their souls?

Five

I<small>N</small> *A.I.: ARTIFICIAL INTELLIGENCE*, STEVEN SPIELBERG'S sci-fi film set in a future where "mechas" and "orgas"—robots and humans—are barely distinguishable, an anxious young woman sits on the edge of a bed as the handsome mecha she has ordered up to service her begins his slick, reassuring patter. Emotions pass across her face: determination, embarrassment, longing, fear. It is as if she's taken a man she met in the bar downstairs up to her hotel room and now she's wondering, Does he think I'm pretty, what if people find out, what if he's a rapist? But he's not thinking anything. He's just a complicated vibrator. She's alone.

~

The perfect replicant, though, would be able to think, like Rachael, Sean Young's character in *Blade Runner;* she just wouldn't know that her thoughts were programmed. Or might she have an inkling once in a while, a sense of something off about herself? Something too automatic, too predictable? But those moments of self-awareness would not tell her what she was; a really good replicant might be programmed to have exactly these momentary twinges of self-doubt. Perhaps she would believe that her engineering is what makes her human.

On the reality TV show *The Swan,* working-class women—with tired, pleasant faces, crooked teeth, nondescript functional bodies—are isolated in what looks like an upscale Marriott hotel, where for three months they are put through an excruciating regimen of crash dieting, exercise, surgery, liposuction, cosmetic dentistry, and, of course, therapy to boost their self-esteem. They emerge, to their families' weepy delight, looking like curiously identical cocktail hostesses. Then, to remind them that they are basically losers after all, they are made to compete against each other in a beauty contest: there can only be one true Swan. Five hundred thousand women applied to go on the show. On *I Want a Famous Face,* twenty-one-year-old twins Mike and Matt Schlepp—could that actually be their last name?—get makeovers to look like Brad Pitt. "We are ugly," says one, matter-of-factly, although they don't look so bad. "And we want to correct that." The following week, twenty-seven-year-old "marketing executive" Mia gets breast implants to look like Britney Spears. With her long blond hair and regular, bland features Mia already looks quite a bit like Britney—in fact, Britney impersonation is her hobby. She takes this avocation seriously and always tries to be upbeat and friendly when kids ask her if she is Britney. "Most people, I'm the closest they'll get to meeting her," she says, so there's a responsibility involved. How close are you to meeting Britney if you meet someone who looks like her? Closer than if you meet someone who doesn't look like her but who is named Britney? Who ate dinner last night in the same restaurant as Britney? Who comes from Brittany?

At the other end of the culture scale, there's the performance artist Orlan, who has had multiple surgeries to acquire specific features from great paintings—the Mona

Lisa's eyebrow bumps, the chin of Botticelli's Venus, the eyes of Gérôme's Psyche. Insert your own critique of Western beauty ideals here. The photos of Orlan's operations are gruesome and bloody and for sale, as is just about every other aspect of her existence. You can even buy vials of her body fat. "I want to make a hole in my body and then close it up," she told the *Los Angeles Times*. Yet the end result of all this arty masochism is surprisingly ordinary. In one picture, Orlan wears a trim black-and-yellow outfit and designer sunglasses; except for her matching Elsa Lanchester fright wig, half black and half yellow, she looks like a well-kept-up French bourgeoise who happens to have a small lump on each temple—scars from an accident? flaps concealing retractable horns? She could be a *Vogue* editor on her way to a fashion shoot or she could be a cyborg about to cook a baby with her infrared vision. Just looking at the photo, it's hard to say.

In Brazil, a veterinarian will perform cosmetic surgery on your dog. Perhaps even animals are becoming less real.

Six

CHILDREN ARE PROUD OF THEIR SCARS. MY DAUGHTER used to love telling how she got each one—the ridge on her lower lip from falling off a runaway horse on her ninth birthday, the white patch on her hip where she scraped herself against the sidewalk trying to leap over a huge pile of trash. Our faces, too, contain our histories, our own and our families'. When I was young I looked more Jewish, like my mother; as I age, my father's side of the family comes out, what I think of as my Appalachian-farm-wife look, the deep-creased hatchety face of the Kentucky Pollitts, in which sometimes I imagine I can see traces of the Mohawk woman, supposedly a princess, who, so the story goes, married a Pollitt at the end of the eighteenth century. A lot of old American families have a tale like that—and all Indian women seem to be princesses in American mythology—but whether or not my family legend is true, it's part of me, like the fleshy pads on my fingers, which I got from my mother and which horrified me as a teenager. They were such tangible proof that I was hers, that she had made my body down to its very tips. I used to try to flatten them with Scotch tape. Would I want to erase that body memory, all those traces of vanished Levines and Balkanskys and Pollitts and Riddifords and Hubbards swirling and floating in the mirror, to be a blank, a swan? Today I'm glad to have those finger pads because they connect me with my mother, like a boxful of old letters or her ring, with its pale blue stone. I like to catch a glimpse in the mirror of those serious Jews and Methodists of a hundred years ago. I like to think about the echoes of them, and of me, in my daughter's face, and the unexplained folds and angles that remind us that we are all made up of recombined bits of ancient ancestors, even if we don't know who they are. The precise pattern of your wrinkles might be the only one on earth that matches that of a Sumerian farmer who raised millet and goats around 3000 B.C. I like to think of him, relaxing with a pot of his wife's home brew and looking up at the stars, which were not quite in the same positions as they are today, but shone no less brightly and mysteriously.

Seven

"I JUST WANT A DIGNIFIED OLD AGE," MY HUSBAND moans comically, shaking his head with its cloud of white hair I find so moving, so beautiful. I've been telling him about the books I've been reading on women and cosmetic surgery, for a review I was supposed to turn in a year and a half ago. Clearly, I am resisting the subject—maybe because when everything is said and done, after all the fancy philosophical treatises about youth and beauty as images of the divine straight from Plato and Dante, as if cosmetic surgery were the practical equivalent of a comp lit dissertation, after all the clever magazine articles about how women's obsession with appearance is all about one-upping each other, what is most of this starving and carving about but accepting that a woman is basically just a body, a body with a rather short shelf life? You can postpone the expiration date if you "work" at it—clever touch, bringing in the Puritan ethic—or if you "have work done," as if the body were some sort of perpetual construction site. But basically you are suffering a lot to please people you can't make suffer nearly as much in return, and disguising that fact from yourself with a lot of twaddle about self-improvement and self-esteem.

～

At least among the pile of books by my desk, the more educated the intended audience, the more ambivalence the author displays. The down-market books are either consumer guides or, like Hope Donahue's *Beautiful Stranger*, first-person accounts of how the author's deep-seated feelings of worthlessness led to a long string of botched operations by manipulative male-chauvinist doctors. Moving up a level, *Beauty Junkies*, by the *New York Times* style-section reporter Alex Kuczynski, is a blend of both: part tour of a booming, underregulated industry and part the account of the author's own "addiction" to beauty treatments, beginning with Botox at age twenty-eight, on through microdermabrasion and eyelid surgery, until a Restylane disaster at thirty-six made her go cold turkey—a cautionary tale undercut by the author's photo on the back flap, in which she looks like a blond goddess of youth and serenity. The high-end texts, all written by academic feminists, are abstract and equivocal. Behind the grinding gears of jargon, you feel the author trapped between her awareness that cosmetic surgery is obviously a sexist practice and her reluctance to criticize anything women do to get by. You sense the reproof to those earlier, censorious feminists in the way these books eschew words like "victim" and "narcissism" and "lacks inner resources." Although popular feminism is all about choices that cannot be judged, in academic feminism you can barely say women have a choice in the first place, since, as Foucault has shown, our very beings, including our self-understandings, are created by forces acting upon us from without, dispersed throughout social relations like oxygen molecules in air. At the same time, any decision women make displays their "agency"—a magical, elusive quality that sounds a lot like the Calvinist notion of free will, only without the moral judgment, because judgment would be ethnocentric, heteronormative, culturally imperialist, and even—aha!—sexist. There seems to be no way in contemporary feminism to tell women to use their famous agency to pull up their socks and say *Screw you.*

It was so much simpler when feminism meant marching in demonstrations and getting divorced—when saying *Screw you* was the whole point. Small breasts were great back in the braless days, riding lightly on your rib cage and not sweaty underneath, where today the scar would run like a thick red zipper. As for face-lifts and liposuction—gross! Pathetic! Insert your own critique of capitalist reification of the female body here. Today, that way of thinking sounds hopelessly naïve and even puritanical. People can change their sex now, and if people can alter something so fundamental about themselves—which may not be so fundamental after all, seeing that they can alter it—and be applauded for demonstrating the socially constructed nature of nature, why not applaud a fifty-year-old woman who wants to perform being thirty-five by having Dr. 90210 slice up her face? Or a 250-pound woman who decides to perform slimness by having the fat surgically drained from her body? Whoa, wait a minute; that's fatphobia. That's buying into the medicalization of a normal variation in body type and pathologizing undisciplined female flesh. That woman is fine—fit, healthy, gorgeous!—exactly as she is. Any women's studies professor will tell you as much, even if she's on a diet herself. At the beginning of the twenty-first century, the overweight and obese are the only people left whom feminists expect to shoulder the flag of the natural and "be themselves."

Eight

Y ET ISN'T THAT WHAT WE WANT, TO BE OURSELVES?
"The self is a generally utilitarian but sometimes deceitful fiction that the brain creates," says my friend Dan, plunking down before me his copy of *The Illusion of Conscious Will,* by Daniel M. Wegner. "You just can't face it. Nobody can." I could ask, If the self is a fiction, who is the "you" who can't face that truth? But why argue? Maybe he's right; the self is a fiction produced by the brain, or a bourgeois-sentimental social construct, or a plot by our DNA to make us more interesting to prospective mates. Maybe it isn't even about us. Maybe what we think of as our self is just nature's way of making sure our cats have someone to open their cans. And maybe our bodies are fictions also, in a way, created by what we do to them. Think of all those women in the 1930s and 1940s who looked like Olivia de Havilland and Rosalind Russell, with marcelled hair and high cheekbones, or, a few years later, like Barbara Stanwyck, with soft round breasts under jewel-necked sweaters. Think of the men leaning forward into the camera, dapper and confident. Not that much time has passed since people like that were everywhere, but no one in the whole world looks like that anymore, or soon will look like us.

~

I didn't let myself go, after all. I lost weight, I colored my gray hair brown, I bought new makeup and new clothes—a pair of red Bruno Magli heels at the Housing Works thrift shop, a pair of green suede boots at the Aerosole store on

Eighth Street. Nothing elaborate, expensive, painful, or embarrassing. Nothing to write a book about. I simply said good-bye to T. S. Eliot and closed the rectory door behind me. The world was right there on the street, where it had always been.

I'm looking at Jill Krementz's famous black-and-white photograph of Iris Murdoch. She's wearing a dark coat with the collar turned up romantically and a silk scarf knotted like a Girl Scout tie through the collar of her shirt. Her hair is straight and messy, with bangs that look as if they'd been hacked at with a bread knife. She has wrinkles under her eyes, her jawline is beginning to soften, and on the inside corner of one eyebrow and on her cheek are two of those small lumps, like pale warts, that have something to do with estrogen and that some women get at menopause. Her features are pleasantly lopsided, like so many English faces, blurry and sensual. She looks a bit like an intelligent potato. She's plain and beautiful, mannish and feminine, withheld and deeply sexual. She could be a female Byron, or a middle-aged British schoolgirl, or a tired mother of five on her way to the shops. She's fifty-two years old.

Photographs let us feel superior. We know what the people in the picture do not: how the story comes out. But Murdoch not only looks as if she's seen and done everything, she looks as if she knows everything too: the decline into dementia, the dreadful end, her afterlife as "Iris," a character in her husband's books about their marriage and in a movie, as played by Judi Dench. Imagine living her life— celebrated novelist, philosopher, Oxford don—and ending up best known as a proof of your husband's devotion and a demonstration of the benefits of home care for the senile! *You think I don't know what will happen to me,* the penetrating eyes and half smile seem to say, *but I do.* Some version of the common fate: age, deterioriation, death. The details don't matter; we needn't get into them. The important thing is to live, to be yourself, this moment, now. To be the captain of your soul, and know that sooner or later the captain goes down with the ship.

ACKNOWLEDGMENTS

I'd like to thank my incomparable editor, Daniel Menaker, for his wit, grace, and patience; my agent, Melanie Jackson, for her guidance and support; and JoAnn Wypijewski and Betsy Reed for their close readings of various portions of the manuscript. I'm also grateful to my husband, Steven Lukes, for reading and listening to multiple drafts and versions and actually seeming to enjoy it, and to my daughter, Sophie Pollitt-Cohen, for allowing me to write about her younger self.

I've changed some names and identifying details to protect the identities of some of the people depicted in these pages. If I inadvertently changed their names to yours, I can only assure you that I didn't mean to do that.

ABOUT THE AUTHOR

KATHA POLLITT is the author of the essay collections *Virginity or Death!, Subject to Debate,* and *Reasonable Creatures* and is a poet, essayist, and columnist for *The Nation.* She has won many prizes and awards for her work, including the National Book Critics Circle Award for her first collection of poems, *Antarctic Traveller,* and two National Magazine Awards for essays and criticism. She lives in New York City.

ABOUT THE TYPE

This book was set in Walbaum, a typeface designed in 1810 by German punch cutter J. E. Walbaum. Walbaum's type is more French than German in appearance. Like Bodoni, it is a classical typeface, yet its openness and slight irregularities give it a human, romantic quality.